Oxford Read and Discover

Exploring Our World

Jacqueline Martin

Contents

Introduction		3
1	Exploring	4
2	Early Explorers	8
3	Exploring the Past	12
4	Deserts	16
5	Rivers and Rainforests	20
6	The Arctic and Antarctic	24
7	Mountains	28
8	Oceans	32
Activities		36
Projects		52
Glossary		54
About *Read and Discover*		56

OXFORD
UNIVERSITY PRESS

OXFORD
UNIVERSITY PRESS

Great Clarendon Street, Oxford OX2 6DP

Oxford University Press is a department of the University of Oxford. It furthers the University's objective of excellence in research, scholarship, and education by publishing worldwide in

Oxford New York

Auckland Cape Town Dar es Salaam Hong Kong Karachi Kuala Lumpur Madrid Melbourne Mexico City Nairobi New Delhi Shanghai Taipei Toronto

With offices in

Argentina Austria Brazil Chile Czech Republic France Greece Guatemala Hungary Italy Japan Poland Portugal Singapore South Korea Switzerland Thailand Turkey Ukraine Vietnam

OXFORD and OXFORD ENGLISH are registered trade marks of Oxford University Press in the UK and in certain other countries

© Oxford University Press 2010

The moral rights of the author have been asserted

Database right Oxford University Press (maker)

First published 2010

2014 2013 2012 2011 2010
10 9 8 7 6 5 4 3 2

No unauthorized photocopying

ISBN: 978 0 19 464500 3

An Audio CD Pack containing this book and a CD is also available, ISBN 978 0 19 464540 9

The CD has a choice of American and British English recordings of the complete text.

An accompanying Activity Book is also available, ISBN 978 0 19 464510 2

Printed in China

This book is printed on paper from certified and well-managed sources.

ACKNOWLEDGEMENTS

Illustrations by: Kelly Kennedy pp.13, 17, 24, 33; Dusan Pavlic/ Beehive Illustration pp.36, 45, 50; Alan Rowe pp.36, 45, 50; Mark Ruffle p.8-9, 38

The Publishers would also like to thank the following for their kind permission to reproduce photographs and other copyright material: Alamy p.3 (North Pole/Bryan & Cherry Alexander Photography, Teotihuacan/aerialarchives.com), 4 (Nature Picture Library), 6 (map/Helene Rogers, GPS/DOZIER Marc/ Hemis), 7 (Sue Cunningham/Worldwide Picture Library), 11 (C.p. Cushing/ClassicStock), 12 (Dennis Hallinan), 15 (Teotihuacan/aerialarchives.com), 16 (Frans Lemmens), 18 (World History Archive), 27 (Classic Image), 30 (Peter Richardson/Robert Harding Picture Library Ltd); The Bridgeman Art Library p.20 (Captain Meriwether Lewis (1774-1809) and William Clark (1770-1838) on their trans-continental expedition from the Missouri to the Pacific Ocean in 1804-06 (oil on canvas), Burnham, Thomas Mickell (1818-66)/Private Collection); Constanza Ceruti p.29 (photo courtesy of Constanza Ceruti/copyright Constanza Ceruti); Corbis pp.14 (dig/Jiao Weiping/XinHua/XinHua Press, Rosetta Stone/Alfredo Dagli Orti/The Picture Desk Ltd), 19 (Ubar/K.M. Westermann), 25 (Galen Rowell), 31 (Stefen Chow/Aurora Photos), 33 (Visuals Unlimited); Getty Images pp.5 (Chien-min Chung), 10 (Hulton Archive), 13 (O. Louis Mazzatenta/National Geographic), 22(EIGHTFISH/The Image Bank), 24 (Gordon Wiltsie/National Geographic); Mary Evans Picture Library p.21 (Mary Kingsley/Mary Evans Picture Library); Meg Lowman p.23; Oxford University Press pp.3 (Everest, rainforest), 15 (rock paintings), 17, 21 (Lake Victoria), 28; Photolibrary p.26 (Robert Peary/Photolibrary); Rick Smolan p.19 (Robyn Davidson); Science Photo Library pp.32 (Alexis Rosenfeld), 34 (Ria Novosti), 35 (Alexis Rosenfeld).

Introduction

Explorers are people who leave their home to discover new places, or to learn new things about people, plants, or animals. To learn more about our world, they go on exciting journeys through forests, across hot or icy deserts, up mountains, or down rivers.

Do you know about any famous explorers?
Do you know what places they explored, and why?
Where are these places?

Now read and discover more about explorers and exploring our world!

1 Exploring

Thousands of years ago, early people knew about only a very small part of the world. Today we know a lot more, and some of our information comes from explorers. Explorers have changed the world!

Why Do People Explore?

Early people traveled around to find food and water. Most explorers travel because they are curious and want to discover new places and to learn new things. Some early explorers hoped to get rich by discovering new plants, animals, or treasures, and by selling them when they got home. Today, explorers travel to have an adventure, to learn more about remote places, to find something new to help science, or maybe to be famous.

Where Do People Explore?

Early explorers wanted to find new places or people. They crossed land and explored deserts, forests, rivers, and mountains. Then they started to explore the oceans. Today, many explorers want to be the first to go somewhere a new way. Some try to find a different route, or look for new ways to travel. Others want to be the youngest, the fastest, or the first to do something, for example, climb a mountain.

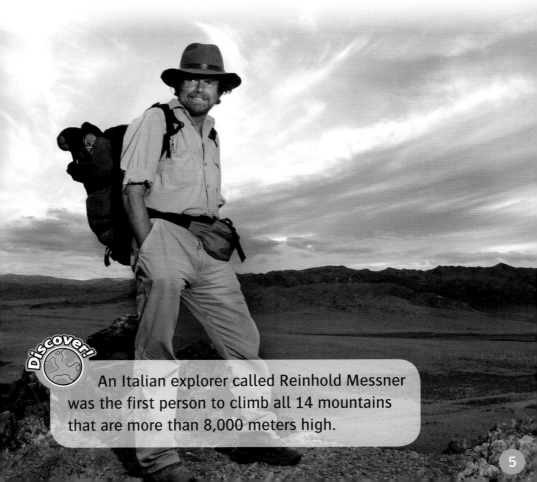

An Italian explorer called Reinhold Messner was the first person to climb all 14 mountains that are more than 8,000 meters high.

How Do People Explore?

Early explorers used only the stars to find their way. Explorers wanted to share what they found, so they wrote about their journeys and made maps. On the maps they drew mountains, rivers, and other things that they had seen, to make it easier for other travelers to follow the same route.

Alexandria

El Faiyum

An Early Map

About 2,200 years ago, Chinese people invented the compass. A compass always points north, so it tells you which direction you are traveling in. GPS instruments that use satellites help modern explorers to find out where they are.

A Modern Explorer Using a GPS Instrument

Why Is Exploring Important?

Information from some early explorers has helped people to make maps to show what the world is like. The things that they wrote tell us what life was like a long time ago in the places that they visited.

Explorers have learned about new plants and animals, discovered new materials, and learned new languages. They have also discovered inventions, and different ways of doing things, for example, new ways of farming.

Scientists in the Amazon Rainforest

Discover!

Modern explorers are still finding new things. Scientists hope that in the future, they will find cures for many diseases in the rainforests and the oceans.

Go to pages 36–37 for activities.

Early Explorers

Early people traveled around to look for food, but they weren't explorers. Explorers go from their home land to discover something about another place, and then they come back and tell people what they found.

Early People

People have lived in most parts of the world for thousands of years. Scientists think that early people started in Africa and traveled to Asia. By about 40,000 years ago, there were people in almost every part of Africa, Asia, and Europe. By about 15,000 years ago they moved into America.

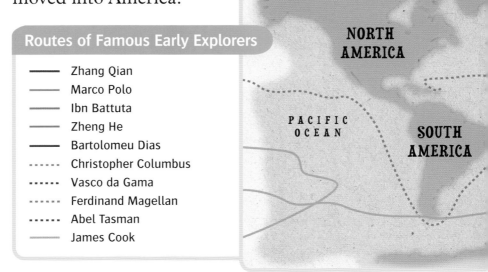

Routes of Famous Early Explorers

— Zhang Qian
— Marco Polo
— Ibn Battuta
— Zheng He
— Bartolomeu Dias
····· Christopher Columbus
····· Vasco da Gama
····· Ferdinand Magellan
····· Abel Tasman
— James Cook

NORTH
AMERICA

PACIFIC
OCEAN

SOUTH
AMERICA

Famous Early Explorers

Zhang Qian was an early explorer from China. He explored many other parts of Asia more than 2,100 years ago. Other people followed his route to trade silk from Asia with things from Europe. The route that he took is now called the Silk Road.

Marco Polo was an explorer from Venice, now in Italy. In 1271, he traveled from Europe to China. When he returned to Italy 24 years later, he told people about inventions like paper, money, pasta, and ice cream.

From about 1325 a Moroccan explorer, Ibn Battuta, explored North Africa, the Middle East, and Asia. He traveled 120,000 kilometers.

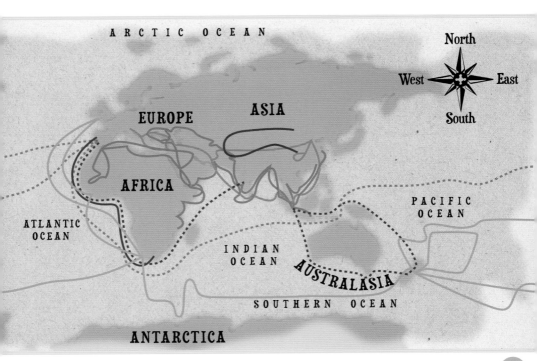

Famous Ocean Explorers

Most early explorers traveled over land, but later, explorers traveled over the ocean. The first explorer to sail from China was Zheng He. In 1405, he sailed south to Indonesia and then across the Indian Ocean and down the east coast of Africa.

A Portuguese explorer, Bartolomeu Dias, was the first explorer to travel west from Europe by ship. In 1488 he sailed from Portugal around the south of Africa. Ten years later another Portuguese explorer, Vasco da Gama, sailed even further and reached India.

Christopher Columbus was an explorer from Genoa, now in Italy. He sailed west from Europe. He reached the West Indies in 1492 and thought he was near India, but he was near a place that no one in Europe knew about – America!

Columbus Arriving in the West Indies

A Portuguese explorer called Ferdinand Magellan was the first explorer to travel to Asia by sailing west from Spain. In 1520 he sailed around South America and across the Pacific Ocean.

Magellan and His Ships

In 1616, some Dutch explorers discovered the west of Australia. In 1642 another Dutch sailor called Abel Tasman discovered New Zealand.

Antarctica was the last continent to be explored. A British sailor called James Cook explored a lot of places. In 1773, he was the first explorer to cross the Antarctic Circle, but he didn't see Antarctica. People think that the first explorers to land on Antarctica were led by a Norwegian explorer called Henryk Bull in 1895.

Go to pages 38–39 for activities.

There are lots of people who explore the past. This helps scientists to understand what is happening on Earth today.

How Earth Was Made

Geologists are scientists who study rocks to learn how Earth was made and how it has changed. They discovered that Earth is made of hot liquid rock that is covered by big pieces of solid rock called plates. The plates can move, and when they crash into each other, they can push up and make a mountain or a volcano, or they can cause an earthquake. Scientists study how the plates move to try to tell when earthquakes will happen or when volcanoes will erupt.

A Volcano Erupting

Plants and Animals in the Past

When ancient plants and animals died, they were buried under sand and mud. After a long time, they went hard and changed into fossils. Paleontologists are scientists who study fossils to learn which plants and animals lived on Earth in the past. They have discovered fossilized plants and bones, teeth, eggs, and shells from fish, birds, insects, and other animals that lived up to 500 million years ago. These discoveries give us information about animals that lived a long time ago – like dinosaurs!

Discover!

Scientists have found fossils of ocean animals at the top of Mount Everest. This means that the rocks on Mount Everest were once under the ocean and were pushed up.

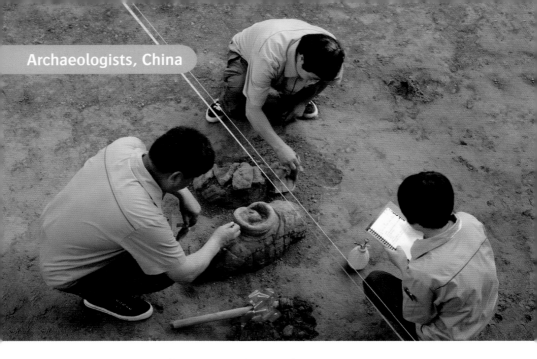

Archaeologists, China

How People Lived in the Past

Archaeologists study ancient places, buildings, bones, or objects, to learn about how people lived in the past. These things tell us what skills and materials people had, what they believed, and what clothes they wore.

Some old buildings, like the Great Wall of China, are easy to see. Sometimes, the things that archaeologists look for have been buried for a long time, and they have to dig them up very carefully.

Discover!

The discovery of the Rosetta Stone in Egypt was very important. It helped people to understand the Ancient Egyptian alphabet and to learn about life in Ancient Egypt.

Teotihuacan, Mexico

Important Discoveries

Many ancient buildings and objects have been found in Central America, for example, in Mexico. By studying these discoveries, archaeologists have learned a lot about how the Mayan people lived about 2,000 years ago, and how the Aztec people lived about 500 years ago.

At Mohenjo Daro, now in Pakistan, archaeologists have found houses from 4,500 years ago with toilets and bathrooms!

Many important discoveries have also been found in caves. In 2009, an archaeologist called Quirino Olivera found cave paintings more than 6,000 years old in the Andes. Cave paintings at Kakadu National Park in Australia tell archaeologists about people and animals who lived there up to 23,000 years ago.

A Cave Painting in Kakadu, Australia

 Go to pages 40–41 for activities.

15

4 Deserts

A desert is an area of land where less than 25 centimeters of rain falls every year. At the moment about 30% of the land on Earth is part of a desert, but deserts are getting bigger.

Different Types of Desert

There are four types of desert. They form in different ways near the equator, near the ocean, near mountains, or inland. Only 25% of deserts are sandy, and the rest are made from stones. All deserts are very dry, but they can be hot or cold. Antarctica is a desert. It's very cold, but it doesn't snow there very often. The largest hot desert in the world is the Sahara Desert in Africa.

The Sahara Desert

Why Do People Explore Deserts?

People have explored deserts for many years. Early desert explorers went to find things to trade, or new trade routes. Not much grows in the desert, but underground there can be salt, oil, gold, or precious stones like diamonds. Today, explorers want to learn about the people who live in deserts, and some just want an adventure!

Archaeologists have found villages buried under the sand. In 1922 an American explorer, Roy Chapman Andrews, found lots of dinosaur bones in the Gobi Desert in Mongolia.

Discover!

Explorers keep discovering new things in the desert because the wind blows the sand around and changes the landscape!

Desert Explorers

Many early desert explorers wanted to be the first to travel all the way across a desert. The first person to travel across the Sahara Desert was a French explorer called René Caillé. In 1828 he traveled across the Sahara with camels because they can walk a long way without food or water.

In 1887 a British explorer, Francis Younghusband, crossed the Gobi Desert in 70 days. The first women explorers to cross the Gobi Desert were British explorers, Mildred Cable, Evangeline French, and Francesca French, who traveled in a mule-cart in about 1926!

The first European explorers went to the coast of Australia, but no one knew what was in the center. In 1860 two British explorers, Robert Burke and William Wills, and an Australian explorer called John King, were the first explorers to cross Australia from the south to the north. They brought camels from India to help them.

Burke, Wills, and King in Australia

Robyn Davidson and Her Camels

The first woman explorer to cross the Australian Desert from east to west was an Australian explorer called Robyn Davidson. In 1977 she traveled 2,735 kilometers by camel from Alice Springs in central Australia to the west coast.

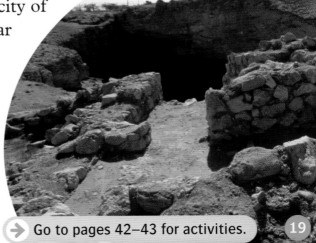

The City of Ubar

In 1992, American scientists discovered the 'lost' city of Ubar on a space radar image. Then some explorers led by a British explorer, Ranulph Fiennes, went to find the city in the desert in Oman.

Go to pages 42–43 for activities.

5 Rivers and Rainforests

Many parts of the world are hard to explore because they are covered by rainforests or mountains. Explorers often travel by river to get to some of these places.

Lewis and Clark Exploring the Missouri River

New Trade Routes

In the past, some governments gave explorers money if they found an easier route to another country, because their country could then earn money by trading things. In 1804, American explorers, Meriwether Lewis and William Clark, explored the Missouri River to look for a new trade route to the Pacific Ocean. It took them 18 months, but they made it! They drew maps and wrote about the things they saw and the people they met. In 1542 a Spanish explorer called Francisco de Orellana sailed down the Amazon River from its source to the Atlantic Ocean. He found lots of new materials to trade.

Mary Kingsley on the Ogowe River, Africa

New Discoveries

In 1895 a British explorer called Mary Kingsley traveled along the Ogowe River in Africa to learn about the people there. She also found many new types of fish!

Lots of river explorers wanted to be the first to find the source – where a river starts. Many explorers have tried to find the source of the Nile River in Africa – the longest river in the world. They have all returned with different ideas.

Lake Victoria

Discover!

Scientists still don't all agree where the source of the Nile is, but most people think that it's Lake Victoria.

A Rainforest in Indonesia

Amazing Rainforests

Rainforests are very important. They only cover 6% of the land on Earth, but more than half of all types of animal and plant on Earth live there. Some rainforest trees have more flowers and fruits than any other trees in the world. Some medicines that we use are made from plants from the rainforests, and scientists think there are lots more plants to be discovered.

Discover!

Sugar, chocolate, coffee, chewing gum, rubber, and many fruits, nuts, and spices come from rainforests.

Rainforest Explorers

Many rainforest explorers are scientists looking for new types of plant or animal. In about 1800 a German explorer, Alexander von Humboldt, and a French explorer, Aimé Bonpland, looked for new plants in the South American rainforests. They returned with new information about people and wildlife.

In 1848 two British explorers, Alfred Russel Wallace and Henry Bates, went to Brazil to look for new insects. Snakes and insects bit them and some people shot at them, but they found 14,712 types of insect including 8,000 new ones!

In the past, explorers only moved along the ground. Today, explorers like this American scientist, Meg Lowman, use special ropes to climb trees and explore the top of the rainforest.

Meg Lowman Exploring a Rainforest

 Go to pages 44–45 for activities.

23

6 The Arctic and Antarctic

The Arctic and Antarctic were the last places to be explored. Early explorers went to see what was there, and later, others went to look for the minerals and ocean animals that were found by early explorers.

Reaching the Poles

Early explorers wanted to be first to reach the ends of the Earth – the Poles. Modern explorers try to get to the Poles more quickly or by using different vehicles, for example, a hot-air balloon.

Discover!

Near the Poles, the sun doesn't go down in summer – this is called the midnight sun.

23:59

What's at the Poles?

The Arctic is like a giant ice cube! There's no land there – just ice and water. The Antarctic has land, too – it's called Antarctica. In the past, the Antarctic was warm. Scientists have found fossils there of the same plants and animals that they have found in Australia and South America. They also found fossils of eight types of dinosaur! Today there are lots of scientific research stations in Antarctica. Scientists study the wildlife, ice, fossils, weather, and climate to help us to understand more about Earth. There are oil, gas, and minerals under both places, but they are hard to get to through the ice.

A Research Station, Antarctica

The Arctic and the North Pole

The first Arctic explorers came from Asia. They wanted to find new land to live on and animals to hunt. The first European explorers arrived in about 1500. They were looking for a shorter trade route to Asia from Europe through the Arctic.

In 1728, a Danish explorer, Vitus Bering, was the first explorer to find the Northeast Passage around Russia. In 1906, a Norwegian explorer, Roald Amundsen, found a way around the top of Alaska – now called the Northwest Passage.

Most people believe that the first explorer to get to the North Pole was an American explorer, Robert Peary, in 1909.

Robert Peary's Team at the North Pole

Roald Amundsen at the South Pole

The Antarctic and the South Pole

Roald Amundsen, and a British explorer, Robert Scott, raced to be first to the South Pole. Amundsen got to the Pole first in December 1911. He used skis and dog sleds, and returned safely with all his men. Scott's men walked, pulling everything on sleds. They got to the Pole a few weeks later and found that Amundsen's Norwegian flag was already there. Sadly, Scott and his team died on the way back.

The first explorers to cross Antarctica were led by a British explorer called Vivian Fuchs in 1958. In 2001 an American explorer, Ann Bancroft, and a Norwegian explorer, Liv Arnesen, were the first women to cross it.

Go to pages 46–47 for activities.

Mountains

Mountains cover about 25% of Earth. They are made of rocks and soil, and they are much higher than the land around them. They form when underground plates crash together and push the land up. This takes millions of years.

Record-Breaking Mountains

The biggest mountain chain is the Himalayas in Asia. Mount Everest, the highest mountain in the world, is in the Himalayas. Everest is still growing about 5 millimeters every year.

The longest mountain chain is under the ocean! The Mid-Atlantic Ridge under the Atlantic Ocean is 16,000 kilometers long. The longest mountain chain on land is the Andes in South America.

The Andes Mountains

Why Do People Explore Mountains?

Geologists look at the rocks in mountains to learn more about how Earth was made. Some mountain explorers have found metals like gold, silver, copper, and tin. They have also found precious stones like rubies and emeralds, and rocks, like granite and limestone. Some mountain plants, like the snow lotus, are used to make medicines.

Mountain archaeologists look for ancient remains on the top of mountains. In 1999, Constanza Ceruti from Argentina was exploring 6,739 meters high at the top of the Llullaillaco Volcano between Argentina and Chile. She and Johan Reinhold found food pots, gold and silver statues, and three Inca mummies that were 500 years old.

Constanza Ceruti, Argentina

Mountain Explorers

Mountain explorers often want to be the first to climb a mountain. A Frenchman called Antoine de Ville climbed Mont Aiguille in the Alps in 1492.

Later, some people gave explorers money to climb mountains to see what was there. Michel Gabriel Paccard and Jacques Balmat climbed Mont Blanc for a prize in 1786. Another French explorer called Marie Paradis was the first woman to climb Mont Blanc in 1808.

The first people to get to the top of Mount Everest were Edmund Hillary from New Zealand and Tenzing Norgay from Nepal in 1953. About 2,000 people have climbed to the top of Everest, but more than 200 of them never returned. Modern explorers try and find new ways to climb it.

The first woman to get to the top of Everest was a Japanese climber called Junko Tabei in 1975. In 1992 she also became the first woman to climb the highest mountain in each of the seven continents.

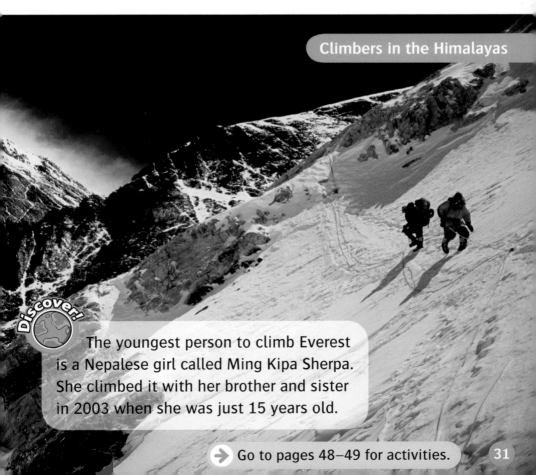

Climbers in the Himalayas

Discover!

The youngest person to climb Everest is a Nepalese girl called Ming Kipa Sherpa. She climbed it with her brother and sister in 2003 when she was just 15 years old.

Go to pages 48–49 for activities.

8 Oceans

After exploring most of the land, people started to explore under the oceans. The oceans are enormous – they cover about 70% of Earth. There are still thousands of kilometers of seabed to be explored.

What Do We Know?

There are five oceans, but more than half of all the water in the oceans is in just one ocean – the Pacific Ocean. At first, scientists thought that the seabed was flat, but now we know that there are mountains, valleys, volcanoes, and plains under the water. By studying the seabed, scientists have learned that the oceans started to form 4,000 million years ago. They have found bones from land animals on the seabed, which shows that the sea level is much higher now.

An Explorer in the Pacific Ocean

What's in the Oceans?

The oceans are full of amazing plants and animals. Some ocean plants, like seaweed, can be used to make medicines. Today, scientists know about 25,000 different types of fish. They find more than 100 new types every year.

There are lots of precious things in the oceans. Pearls are jewels that can form inside oyster shells. There are metals like gold, iron, and copper in the seabed, too. More than 20% of all the oil that we use comes from under the oceans.

Discover!

There's enough salt in the oceans to cover Earth with up to 150 meters of salt.

Ocean Explorers

Early ocean explorers could only explore for as long as they could breathe. In 1943, two Frenchmen, Jacques Cousteau and Emile Gagnan, invented Self Contained Underwater Breathing Apparatus (SCUBA). This allowed divers to stay underwater for longer and dive deeper than ever before.

In 1960, a Swiss explorer, Jacques Piccard, and an American, Don Walsh, dived down almost 11 kilometers in a small submarine to the deepest part of the Pacific Ocean. It's the deepest that anyone has dived. No one thought anything could live that far down, but they found some new types of fish.

An American explorer called Silvia Alice Earle holds the record for the deepest woman diver in a submersible. She has spent more than 7,000 hours underwater.

Ocean Explorers Using a Submersible

A Robot on the Seabed

What Next?

Modern explorers have better equipment and they can explore further than ever before, but they don't even have to go anywhere. Today we can send robots to explore places and bring back information!

The oceans are the least explored part of Earth, but there are still things to find in rainforests, mountains to climb, and thousands of places to explore. What part of our world would you like to explore?

→ Go to pages 50–51 for activities.

1 **Exploring**

← Read pages 4–7.

1 **Write the words.**

> river   map   ~~mountain~~
> forest   compass   satellite

1 __mountain__

2 _____

3 _____

4 _____

5 _____

6 _____

2 **Write *true* or *false*.**

1 Explorers have changed the world.   __true__

2 Early people traveled to find food.   _____

3 Explorers aren't curious.   _____

4 Explorers want to discover new places.   _____

5 Some early explorers hoped to get sick.   _____

6 Some early explorers wanted to find new   _____
things to sell.

7 Some explorers want to be last to find   _____
something.

8 Some explorers want to be famous.   _____

3 **Order the words.**

1 explorers / Early / find / new / wanted /to / places.

   Early explorers wanted to find new places.

2 deserts, / They / mountains. / explored / rivers, / and

   _____

3 land / They / crossed / oceans. / and / explored

   _____

4 to / want / new / somewhere / a / Explorers / go / way.

   _____

5 travel. / Some / look / ways / for / new / explorers / to

   _____

6 be / Others / to / want / something. / the / to / fastest / do

   _____

4 **Complete the sentences.**

> instruments   maps   mountains
> stars   rivers   compass   north

1 Early explorers used the _____stars_____ to find their way.

2 Explorers wrote about their journeys and made _____.

3 They drew _____ and _____ on the maps.

4 About 2,200 years ago Chinese people invented the

   _____.

5 A compass always points _____.

6 Modern explorers can use GPS _____.

2 Early Explorers

← Read pages 8–11.

1 **Write the words.**

Antarctica   North America   Asia
Africa   Atlantic Ocean   Pacific Ocean
Europe   South America   Indian Ocean

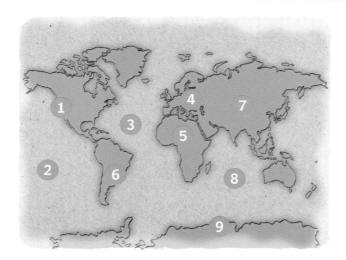

1 _____

2 _____

3 _____

4 _____

5 _____

6 _____

7 _____

8 _____

9 _____

2 **Correct the sentences.**

1 Early people traveled around to look for rocks.

   Early people traveled around to look for food.

2 Zhang Qian was an early explorer from Europe.

   _____

3 Marco Polo traveled from Africa to China.

   _____

4 Ibn Battuta explored North America, the Middle East, and Asia.

   _____

3 Match. Then write complete sentences.

1405	Vasco da Gama	from Europe to Asia
1488	Ferdinand Magellan	to New Zealand
1492	Abel Tasman	to the Antarctic
1498	Zheng He	from Europe to India
1520	James Cook	from China to East Africa
1642	Bartolomeu Dias	from Europe to America
1773	Henryk Bull	from Europe to Africa
1895	Christopher Columbus	to Antarctica

1 In 1405, Zheng He traveled from China to East Africa.

2 _____

3 _____

4 _____

5 _____

6 _____

7 _____

8 _____

4 Which explorer do you think was the most important? Why? _____

_____

_____

_____

_____

③ Exploring the Past

← Read pages 12–15.

1 Circle the correct words.

1 Exploring the past helps scientists to **read** / **understand**
what is happening today.

2 Geologists study **weather** / **rocks** to learn how Earth
was made.

3 Earth is made of pieces of solid rock called **cups** / **plates**.

4 When the plates crash they can cause **an earthquake** /
a storm.

5 Paleontologists study **buildings** / **fossils** to learn about
plants and animals in the past.

6 Fossils give us information about plants and **plates** /
animals from a long time ago.

2 Complete the sentences.

> explore the past   make a mountain   on Mount Everest
> earthquakes will happen   under the ocean

1 There are lots of people who _____ .

2 When plates crash, they push up and _____ .

3 Scientists study plates to tell when _____ .

4 Paleontologists have discovered fossils _____ .

5 The rocks on Mount Everest were once _____ .

3 Complete the chart.

> wore   made   fossils   ~~geologists~~   rocks
> archaeologists   animals   paleontologists

Who?	What do they find or study?	What does this tell us?
geologists	_____	how Earth was _____ and how it changed
_____	_____	which plants and _____ lived a long time ago
_____	ancient buildings or objects	what people did, believed, and _____

4 Answer the questions.

1 What did the Rosetta Stone help people to understand?

It helped them to understand the Ancient Egyptian alphabet.

2 Where was the Rosetta Stone found?

_____

3 What have archaeologists learned from ancient buildings in Mexico?

_____

4 How old were the houses found in Mohenjo Daro?

_____

5 What have archaeologists found in Kakadu National Park?

_____

6 Where did Quirino Olivera find paintings?

_____

(4) Deserts

← Read pages 16–19.

1 Complete the sentences.

1 At the moment about __30%__ of the land on Earth is part of a desert. (30% / 50%)

2 A desert is an area of land where _____ than 25 centimeters of rain falls every year. (less / more)

3 Deserts are getting _____. (smaller / bigger)

4 There are _____ types of desert. (four / five)

5 Only 25% of deserts are _____. (rocky / sandy)

6 All deserts are _____, but they can be hot or cold. (dry / wet)

7 The largest _____ desert in the world is the Sahara Desert. (cold / hot)

2 Match.

1 People have explored deserts	under deserts.
2 Some early desert explorers went to	buried under the sand.
3 Some explorers want to learn	dinosaur bones in the Gobi Desert.
4 Some explorers want	for many years.
5 There can be salt, oil, or gold	find new trade routes.
6 Archaeologists have found villages	about the people who live in deserts.
7 An American explorer found	an adventure.

3 **Correct the sentences.**

1 Many early desert explorers went to find deserts to trade.

_____

2 René Caillé traveled across the Sahara Desert by train.

_____

3 Camels can walk a long way without food or clothes.

_____

4 Francis Younghusband crossed the Australian Desert.

_____

5 Robyn Davidson crossed the Sahara Desert in 1977.

_____

4 **Complete the chart.**

new famous lost hot

Good things about being a desert explorer:	Bad things about being a desert explorer:
you could find something _____	it's easy to get _____
you could become _____	it's very _____ or very cold

5 **Would you like to be a desert explorer? Why / Why not?**

_____

_____

_____

5 Rivers and Rainforests

← Read pages 20–23.

1 Write *true* or *false*.

1 Countries can earn money by trading things with each other. _____

2 Governments sometimes gave explorers food if they found a new route. _____

3 Lots of explorers wanted to be the first to find the source of a river. _____

4 The River Nile is the longest river in the world. _____

2 Complete the sentences.

land   rainforest   flowers   climb   discover   plants

1 Rainforests cover 6% of the _____ on Earth.

2 More than half of the animals and _____ on Earth live in rainforests.

3 Rainforest trees have more fruits and _____ than other trees.

4 Some medicines are made from _____ plants.

5 Scientists think that there are more plants to _____ .

6 Modern rainforest explorers use special ropes to _____ the trees.

3 Find and write the words.

s	m	s	p	i	c	e	s	o	r
p	e	a	r	t	a	x	n	b	u
e	d	k	a	u	t	e	g	n	b
s	i	l	d	t	c	l	t	u	b
u	c	h	o	c	o	l	a	t	e
g	i	c	o	e	f	f	v	s	r
a	n	h	p	w	f	r	u	i	t
r	e	o	s	s	e	a	t	m	s
o	s	b	i	o	e	r	s	o	o
c	h	e	w	i	n	g	g	u	m

1 ___spices___   2 _____   3 _____

4 _____   5 _____   6 _____

7 _____   8 _____   9 _____

4 Answer the questions.

1 What are many rainforest explorers looking for?

_____

2 Which river did Meriwether Lewis and William Clark explore? Where is it?

_____

3 What did Mary Kingsley find in the Ogowe River?

_____

4 What did Alfred Russel Wallace and Henry Bates find in Brazil?

_____

6 The Arctic and Antarctic

← Read pages 24–27.

1 Complete the sentences.

see   quickly   minerals
Antarctic   ends   vehicles

1 The Arctic and _____ were the last places to be explored.

2 Early explorers went to _____ what was there.

3 Later, other explorers went to look for _____ and ocean animals.

4 Early explorers wanted to be first to reach the _____ of the Earth.

5 Modern explorers try to get to the Poles more _____ or by using different _____ .

2 Write *Arctic* or *Antarctic*.

1 In the past, it was warm. _____

2 It has land. _____

3 It's like a giant ice cube. _____

4 Scientists have found fossils there. _____

5 The first explorers went there from Asia. _____

6 There are lots of research stations there today. _____

7 The North Pole is there. _____

8 The South Pole is there. _____

3 Match. Then write complete sentences.

1500	Vivian Fuchs	found the Northwest Passage
1728	Roald Amundsen	crossed Antarctica
1906	European explorers	were the first women to cross Antarctica
1909	Robert Peary	reached the Arctic
1911	Roald Amundsen	sailed into the Northeast Passage
1958	Ann Bancroft and Liv Arnesen	reached the South Pole
2001	Vitus Bering	reached the North Pole

1 _____

2 _____

3 _____

4 _____

5 _____

6 _____

7 _____

4 Would you like to be a polar explorer? Which Pole would you visit? Why / Why not?

_____

_____

_____

_____

7 Mountains

← Read pages 28–31.

1 Correct the sentences.

1 Mountains are lower than the land around them.

_____

2 Mountains cover about 50% of Earth.

_____

3 The smallest mountain chain is the Himalayas.

_____

4 Mount Everest is growing about 5 millimeters every week.

_____

5 The Mid-Atlantic Ridge is under the Pacific Ocean.

_____

6 The tallest mountain chain on land is the Andes.

_____

2 Why do explorers climb mountains? Write four answers.

1 _____

2 _____

3 _____

4 _____

3 Complete the sentences.

1 Explorers have found precious _____ in some mountains. (stones / money)

2 Some mountain plants are used to make _____ . (medicines / clothes)

3 Marie Paradis was the _____ woman to climb Mont Blanc. (first / last)

4 About 2,000 _____ have climbed to the top of Mount Everest. (people / fish)

5 Junko Tabei was the first woman to climb the _____ mountain in each continent. (shortest / highest)

4 Complete the chart.

Mont Aiguille Ming Kipa Sherpa Edmund Hillary volcano
Mont Blanc 1808 Everest Gabriel Paccard 1975

Year	Explorer	Mountain Fact
1492	Antoine de Ville	first person to climb _____
1786	_____ and Jacques Balmat	climbed _____ for a prize
1953	_____ and Tenzing Norgay	first people to reach the top of Everest
_____	Junko Tabei	first woman to climb _____
1999	Constanza Ceruti	found Inca mummies at the top of a _____
2003	_____	youngest person to climb Everest

8 Oceans

1 Circle the correct words.

1 The oceans are **enormous** / **famous**.

2 There are **five** / **seven** oceans.

3 More than **half** / **a quarter** of the water is in the Pacific Ocean.

4 At first, scientists thought that the seabed was **round** / **flat**.

5 There are mountains, valleys, and **plains** / **planes** under the water.

6 Sea level is **higher** / **lower** now than in the past.

2 Complete the sentences.

1 More than 20% of all the _____ that we use comes from the oceans.

2 There's enough _____ in the oceans to cover Earth up to 150 meters.

3 _____ are jewels that can form inside oyster shells.

4 Today, scientists know about 25,000 types of _____ in the oceans.

5 There are metals like gold, _____ , and copper in the seabed.

6 Some ocean plants, like _____ , can be used to make medicines.

3 **Order the words.**

1 Oceans / full / are / animals. / of / plants / amazing /and

_____

2 more / 100 / Scientists / new / find / of / year. / fish / every / types / than

_____

3 explore / for / Early / long / as / explorers / could / only / ocean / could / as / they / breathe.

_____

4 1960 / explorers / In / dived / two / to / deepest / the / of / Pacific / part / the / Ocean.

_____

4 **Answer the questions.**

1 What did Jacques Piccard and Don Walsh dive in?

_____

2 What did they find?

_____

3 How long has Silvia Alice Earle spent underwater?

_____

4 Why don't modern explorers have to go anywhere?

_____

5 **Where would you like to explore and why?**

_____

_____

Famous Places

1 These places have the same name as the explorers who found them. Look in books or on the Internet and find out where they are.

> Cook Islands   Bering Strait   Tasmania

2 Write notes about the explorers who found these places.

James Cook _____

_____

_____

_____

Vitus Bering _____

_____

_____

_____

Abel Tasman _____

_____

_____

_____

3 Do you know any other places that have the same name as a famous explorer? Are there any in your country?

4 Write about the places and display your work.

An Exploring Poster

1 **Choose one type of place, for example, deserts or rainforests.**

2 **Look in books or on the Internet. Write notes about this type of place.**

Where in the world is this type of place?

What can explorers find there?

Type of Place

Which explorers have explored this type of place? Where? When? What did they find?

3 **Make a poster about this type of place. Write sentences and add pictures, maps, and photos. Display your poster.**

Glossary

agree to think the same thing

allow to make something possible

ancient from thousands of years in the past

archaeologist someone who studies history, by looking at ancient objects

area a part of a place

become to change into; to start to be

believe to think that something is true

bite to break something with your teeth

blow to move with the wind

bone the hard part of a skeleton

breathe to take in and let out air through your nose and mouth

bury to put a person into the ground when they are not living any more

cause to make something happen

center the middle

chain a line of mountains

change to become different; to make something different

climate the usual type of weather in a country

coast the land next to the sea or ocean

coffee a hot drink made from coffee beans

cover to put something over something; to be over something

cross to move from one side to another

cure something that makes a medical problem go away

curious wanting to know more about something

deep going a long way down

die to stop living

dig up to get something out of the ground

dinosaur an animal that lived millions of years ago

disease a medical problem that makes you very sick

dive to swim underwater

earn to get money for work that you do

earthquake when the ground moves

end the part of a thing that is farthest from the center

enormous very big

equipment things that help you to do something

famous known by many people

flag a piece of material with a special design for a country

forest a place with a lot of trees

form to make or be made

fruit the part of a plant that has a stone or seeds

further a longer way

gas not a solid or liquid; like air

gold an expensive yellow metal

ground the land that we stand on

grow to get bigger

half one of two parts

hot-air balloon a balloon that people can fly in

hunt to try to catch animals to kill them

ice cube a small, square piece of ice used to make drinks cold

inland far from the ocean

insect a very small animal with six legs

invent to make or design something new

jewel a precious stone

land when a plane or boat touches the land

landscape what the land is like

language the words that people speak and write

lead to be the first in a group

liquid not a solid or gas; like water

material something that we use to make other things

medicine something that you take when you are sick, to make you better

metal a hard material made from minerals

mineral a material, like gold or salt, that's in the ground

modern not from the past

move to go from one place to another

mule-cart a vehicle that is pulled by an animal like a horse

mummy (*plural* **mummies**) a dead body covered with soft material

object a thing

ocean the salt water that covers most of Earth

oil a fuel; it's a black liquid used to make gasoline

oyster an ocean animal with a shell

past many years ago

plain a large area of flat land

precious special and expensive

prize something you get when you win

push to make something move away; the opposite of pull

race to try and go somewhere faster than someone else

record for example, the best or highest thing that there is

remains parts of ancient objects

remote far from other places

return to come back

river water on land that goes to the ocean

robot a machine that is moved by a computer

rock a very hard, natural material

route the way you go to get from one place to another

rubber a soft material that you use to make tires

safely not being damaged

satellite a machine that goes into space

seabed the floor of the ocean

sea level how high the water is in the sea or ocean

shell the hard, outside part of an egg or of some animals

ship a large boat

shoot to use a gun

silk a soft material that is used to make clothes

skill something someone can do well

sled a vehicle that travels over snow

snake an animal with a thin body and no legs

solid not a liquid or gas; like hard rock

special different and important

spend to use time doing something

spice seeds or powder from plants that we use to give taste to food

statue a shape of a person or animal made of stone or metal

stone a very hard, natural material

submarine a ship that can travel underwater

top the highest part

trade to buy and sell things

treasure a special, expensive object

valley the land between hills or mountains

vehicle something for moving goods or people

village a few houses in the countryside; smaller than a town

without not having something; not doing something

Oxford Read and Discover

Series Editor: Hazel Geatches • CLIL Adviser: John Clegg

Oxford Read and Discover graded readers are at four levels, from 3 to 6, suitable for students from age 8 and older. They cover many topics within three subject areas, and can support English across the curriculum, or Content and Language Integrated Learning (CLIL).

Available for each reader:
• Audio CD Pack (book & audio CD)
• Activity Book

For Teacher's Notes & CLIL Guidance go to
www.oup.com/elt/teacher/readanddiscover

Subject Area / Level	The World of Science & Technology	The Natural World	The World of Arts & Social Studies
3 600 headwords	• How We Make Products • Sound and Music • Super Structures • Your Five Senses	• Amazing Minibeasts • Animals in the Air • Life in Rainforests • Wonderful Water	• Festivals Around the World • Free Time Around the World
4 750 headwords	• All About Plants • How to Stay Healthy • Machines Then and Now • Why We Recycle	• All About Desert Life • All About Ocean Life • Animals at Night • Incredible Earth	• Animals in Art • Wonders of the Past
5 900 headwords	• Materials to Products • Medicine Then and Now • Transportation Then and Now • Wild Weather	• All About Islands • Animal Life Cycles • Exploring Our World • Great Migrations	• Homes Around the World • Our World in Art
6 1,050 headwords	• Cells and Microbes • Clothes Then and Now • Incredible Energy • Your Amazing Body	• All About Space • Caring for Our Planet • Earth Then and Now • Wonderful Ecosystems	• Helping Around the World • Food Around the World

For younger students, **Dolphin Readers** Levels Starter, 1, and 2 are available.

BETWEEN

TIDES

(*Entre les Eaux*) by

V. Y. Mudimbe

translated from the French by

Stephen Becker

SIMON & SCHUSTER

New York   London   Toronto   Sydney   Tokyo   Singapore

SIMON & SCHUSTER
Simon & Schuster Building
Rockefeller Center
1230 Avenue of the Americas
New York, New York 10020

Designed by Caroline Cunningham
Manufactured in the United States of America

10 9 8 7 6 5 4 3 2 1

Library of Congress Cataloging in Publication data

Mudimbe, V. Y., date
    [Entre les eaux. English]
    Between tides / V.Y. Mudimbe.
        p.   cm.
    Translation of: Entre les eaux.
    I. Title.
    PQ3989.2.M77E513   1991
    843—dc20   91-19938
                                                  CIP
ISBN: 0-671-73858-5

For Elisabeth

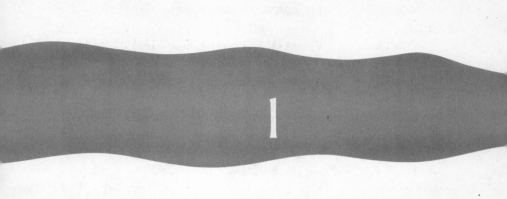

1

WHENEVER MY EYES TURN TO the earthen wall of the barracks and pause at my lucky crucifix, hidden in the withes, I feel like making a monstrous face. Just a tic? Or is it some new emotion taking possession of me? But the reaction is automatic, and is always followed by a rising gorge, a foul new horror, the horror of physical decay. And then the unstated disgust, causeless and effectless, that is coupled with the memory of my masters in Rome. The Angelicum suffused by hot sunshine. Summer's shimmering humidity, to welcome us back from vacation. The exalted voice of Monsignor Sanguinetti, suffocating piously: God is within you, and you are gods. Think of Saint Paul! Indeed . . . You are the Christ. Contemplate the exemplars of faith. Louis of Gonzaga spent hours at a time staring at his crucifix. Dominique Savio so closely identified himself with our Lord. . . . That morning fly, buzzing and flitting, what a disturbing whiff of freedom, of careless joy, in this exhausted barracks! Joy. No: Sanguinetti is my cross. Here he is again: Theresa of Avila never entered or left a room without a glance

at the crucified Christ. Surely you know that Saint John of the
Cross . . .

My God, but I feel more and more remote from them! How
did those joyful saints transcend themselves? Become *other*? Identify themselves so perfectly with love? Is it my time or my place
that is slowly killing me? I feel so alone! For years now I've stared
at one crucifix after another; no use; the same silence always.
They were wooden, iron, plaster, but there was always the same
discouraging distance, affirming separation, deepening my bachelor's solitude. Of the symbol of my faith that I've hidden in
shame among the withes, I see only two small sticks that I've
crossed and set in the thatch that beards the upper wall. Yet they
should mean so much more to me! Otherwise why would I have
created them? I want to believe, and I do believe, as I have all
along, that my strength begins there.

Sanguinetti never wearied of saying, "The saints were not
imaginative." How can I believe that? I always thought that with
more imagination I could approach them. At the very least I
could feel closer to humankind. I'd suffer less if I could create a
communion of suffering, sharing others' joys and sorrows.

Sanguinetti was categorical: Beware imagination! A handsome man he was. The grace of his gestures, the tenderness in his
eyes belying their constant gleam of gentle malice, the unctu-
ousness of his contrived sentences. They were obviously wrought,
intended to strike home. Sometimes the peremptory affirmation
by an incisive, brief phrase: Christ, our salvation; Christ, our
guide. I long envied that firm conviction, that unflagging certainty. I emulated him. But did Sanguinetti's seductive peace fall
upon me even once? For years I tried to live by the rituals of holy
orders. Only my belly was really at peace. Often I approached
the joy of a true priestly calling, only to realize that I had taken
many small liberties with my ideals.

And now I wonder if my faith and my past life have not
been too easy. If I have merely been serving an enormous de-
ception, as my new comrades insist. No. That, I know, cannot

be possible. Well then, all these people so *convinced*—what do they do, to become so sure? Sanguinetti with his dazzling proofs; my new friends with equally evident truths . . . Don't think about it. Don't think at all. Go back to sleep. At least try.

Only I can't. I bore myself with myself whenever I have nothing else to do. Soon it will be six o'clock. I shall be freed at last from my nightly hell. I've tried to conquer insomnia, simply to reject it; but at the moment the *nkusu*—a local flea—are winning. They drove me crazy for a while; I scratched wildly and roused my bunkmates to furious protest. So I accepted my *nkusu*, at first as mortification of the flesh. But for some time now these tiny pinpricks have afforded me an unspeakable pleasure. I quiver voluptuously and wait impatiently for these little bites to reach various parts of my body; their gentle, transient glow spreads and prickles for several seconds, and before one dies away, a thousand more flare up all over me. I twist and turn under the countless dry burns before I finally drift off in the wee small hours. Waking later, I immediately renew what I consider a minor participation in the divine stigmata. How can I cure myself of this sin, which I welcome? In my candor I repeat the psalms, or Father Duval's songs. They increase my pleasure. Can my real mortification be that I am condemned to ecstasy despite myself?

I glance at my watch: one minute after six. At this moment many of my colleagues in the priesthood are celebrating the Mass. My own has been reduced to a quick glimpse of a crucifix nested in the thatch, while my body trembles in lunatic joy. *Hodie, si vocem ejus audieritis, nolite obdurare corda vestra.* . . . Today, if you hear His voice, do not harden your hearts. . . .

It will soon be ten years, and still I listen lovingly, vainly for the sound of that voice. Ten years of silence. Yes, of course there was an exaltation the morning I was ordained, the intoxicating fervor of my first open celebration of the Mass, the public ritual of Holy Mother Church. Fitness was important that day in all ways. The chasuble, a carapace striped silver and gold, lay heavy on my shoulders. The pungent odor of incense mingled with the subtler aroma of candles, and wove itself into the all-embracing rhythm of the choir's chant. The ritual algebra, magically expressed and resolved by the deacon and subdeacon, living dalmatics seamed in gold thread, dizzied me. My poise was shattered by the rites I had dreamed of for years. And Sanguinetti, with his arms flung high and his gaze dissolving heavenward, flooded the little side chapel of Saint Ambrose with pious loquacity. I recall his surprising preamble. He quoted Virgil—Mantua, with its snow-white swans on the grassy-banked river, where springs ran clear and cool, where the lush meadows teemed with lambs. As usual, his metaphors were strung like beads. He held the Cross high. The universality of the message. The boy from Africa. The Mantuan family who had defrayed my student's expenses in Rome and thus helped me climb the steps to this altar. The meaning of the sacrifice offered in that Milanese basilica. How many shared the occasion? My sponsor, Signor Bonacolsi, a professor at the university, sat in the first row. His family. Certain of his colleagues. A number of his students. My countrymen and fellow scholars in Rome and a few of my friends from the Angelicum. My brother, in our civil service at Brussels, had arrived the night before. I had broken into tears at that heartfelt display of piety. And the *Orate fratres* sprang from my lips like a desperate cry for help.

Since then my agony has been the futile effort to relive that communion. To transform myself so that He would speak to me. Only once: Rome, in the Via Merulana. I was waiting for a friend. A voice surged from deep within me. Was I talking to myself? I rejoiced. The fire of that one encounter quickened me for a time against my growing lassitude. Did I not tempt Him in seeking Him out, when he had been calling me by name throughout eternity?

In this barracks crowded with sleepers, a room brightening slowly in the first light, once again a dream dies away, a dream that I revive each morning. My priesthood seems to be reduced to this dreadful interrogation that begins each day so mournfully while my body sweats beneath the *nkusu*'s tender bites. What did Saint Lawrence suffer on his grid?

The dormitory is coming to life. Comrades stretch and yawn. In a few minutes the whistle will shrill. Reveille in a world I am trying to grow used to: the world of a dream almost obscene yet informed by charity. Incongruous? Is not all truth incongruous? My grandmother introduced me to these same dreams: In the time when the skies were the earth, the world was only one great egg. Pietshi, the first man, lived happily with his woman, Kabeya. Their two children were the moon and the sun, who quarreled so often that Kabeya, their mother, died of grief. The egg burst. The sun and moon shared out their hours of dominion. Pietshi damned them and died exhausted. Of his head was created the earth, of his hair the plants, of his flesh the animals, of his blood the rivers, of his bones the mountains, of his nails the stars to reconcile the enemy brothers, and his heart gave birth to a new race of men.

I examine my own universe. These bodies, curled and cramped all night, are stretching and unfolding. All these infallible creatures—pure. Why am I persuaded that they are purer than others? What proof have I, after all?

For two weeks I have been meditating on purity, to calm the restlessness stimulated by leaves rustling outside in the breeze. On purity, and on the discipline of silence they respect so scrupulously. These men formed by hatred, divided by everything but their common resentment of social injustice—how, in their diversity, have they learned to be human sacrifices to justice? What a change from the atmosphere of the seminary! Our little tricks, to steal a forbidden chat in the morning silence: the misplaced toothbrush, the empty tube of toothpaste, the unpolished shoes . . .

The whistle. My watch says six-fifteen. We salute the flag. Exercise. In formation, a silent lope to the river in the valley, two miles from camp. A bath in the cold water. The run back, still in silence. Assembly. Recreation. And at seven o'clock, classes. No breakfast. The first day, surprised, I'd asked my neighbor, "Don't they eat breakfast here?"

"Breakfast is for the middle classes," he answered dryly. "You're not in Charlesville."

I got used to it. We can get used to anything. At home, in my village, we ate once a day, toward the end of the afternoon, when the grown-ups came home from the fields. That seemed so natural to me, so logical, that when I entered the preparatory seminary I was shocked: four meals a day! What hypocritical mockery we fired off at those reverend Flemish fathers who were literally fattening us for the future! The priesthood? A profession for pigs, said my fellow student Jacques Matani. And he adapted to it so gracefully! This very day he is doubtless settled peacefully in his parish, his shameless corpulence ambling punctually to the chapel, his office, and the sacred dining room.

Doing without breakfast is no problem for me now. I grew used to it as to so many other things: not seeing heads bow at my passage; being pushed around and disciplined like any recruit; being insulted for selling out to colonialism and the Vatican's interests. At first I reacted to all that scorn and intolerance with pain and resentment, but now no vein swells at my temple, not at the most truculent obscenity or the most undeserved insult. I believe I've learned self-control—suppressed all the clerical self-importance I learned in Rome. After all, I'm living on nerve. At times my veins seem to run with hot lava. Can it be shame? I can imagine all too clearly my schoolmates' comments, those who did not stray from the straight and narrow: a doctor of Theology, with a degree in Canon Law too, fallen so low! Could I still look them in the eye?

When will I be cured of these futile reactions—to a religion already compromised by its own defenders? Jitters. Anger. The camp's male nurse told me a couple of days ago that my headaches were probably a result of the insomnia; most likely of that suppressed anger too. And this interminable wait. Two weeks now since I volunteered, escaped to the bush to join men and women fighting the established order—or rather the consecrated and approved disorder. My rebellion was a return to the fold: I was rejoining those who cared. I thought I could be useful to them. My degrees and academic titles, the prestigious aura. To help them define their revolution so that its truths might not degenerate for no reason into counterproductive countertruths; so that the violence of our struggle for justice might be based on a revolutionary theology that we could work out together even as we personified that violent justice. As soon as I arrived they promised me a meeting with the colonel. Obviously he has forgotten me, or has no desire to see me. I am merely a number like all the others. I have no part to play in strategies and tactics. Deep down I cannot accept relegation to a "number" in this armed struggle. Yet I must accept it. Yet again, in the name of what solemn duty can I tolerate being only number 134 in the "Serpent Group"?

The camp comprises three combat groups: Lion, commanded directly by the Colonel; Jackal, under the orders of a former Catholic schoolmaster; and my group, gathered around the Serpent's banner and commanded by a tough little bloodshot shrimp called—I have no idea why—Bidoule. The name means nothing, and is faintly silly.

We take classes with an instructor. A demagogue. A thin, chanting eunuch's voice. Theoretically his job is to lecture us on the sociology of colonial societies. He joined up to make war on the revisionists, the unreliable elements. Traitors, with their misreadings of Marx. He gives me the willies. Who here understands him? My fellow students take notes.

Like an oracle this teacher remakes the world: In *Imperialism, the Last Stage of Capitalism*, Lenin opens his analysis with a brilliant summary of imperialism's five fundamental stages: (1) concentration of capital and the means of production so extreme that it creates monopolies whose role in the economy is decisive; (2) amalgamation of banking capital and industrial capital, creating a sufficient capital base for a financial oligarchy; (3) export of consumer goods takes on special importance; (4) formation of monopolistic consortiums to rule spheres of interest; and (5) final partition of the entire globe among the largest capitalist powers. "Our analysis will demonstrate that . . ."

I'm bored stiff. It isn't jealousy. The facile arguments are frightening, but fear gives way to indifference. Paradoxically, I'd be far less sure of myself here and now in this sort of analysis than when I scandalized my fellow seminarians by my interest in Marxism. My professor here seems to give brilliant recitations of dogma too self-evident, in his view, to require logical exposition. Is that a strength? Good Lord, socialist economic theory has to derive primarily from purely abstract concepts, like any body of knowledge. But isn't Marxism—can't Marxism be—both a scientific explanation of economics and far, far more? Limited to producing abstract definitions, adducing only mainspring concepts like the means of production, creating a structure of abstract combinations—how can anyone learn about the day-to-day workings, the human aspirations, of socialism in action? Can you impose lectures which completely ignore that aspect and still defend a socialism whose aim is to transform the inhuman relations of capitalist societies to truly human relations?

If he were free to think matters through, our oracle might raise these questions. But he is a conscientious incarnation of the Invisible Consensus guiding this camp. In Charlesville the newspapers report that Chinese ideologues are training and arming us. I haven't seen one yet. My "professor's" dogmatism perturbs me sufficiently. He is never really himself, this poor fellow, except when he prates about the massacre of the bourgeoisie. That too Marx and Lenin taught him. The cheerful idiot! What is this strange passion for rational rigor in justifying the noblest and most generous impulses of the heart?

Weariness. Despondency. Slogans sanctify acts that in other circumstances we might not consider hopeful. How can we accept this pretty patchwork of murderous phrases, hiding their freight of corpses? I would like to hear words that sprang from naked reality! Once again I measure the gap between them and me. Echoes—which long since ceased to rouse me—fade in my ears: the positive nature of violence, the dialectic of history, the ineluctable application of the historical law of thesis and antithesis. The bloodshed for ideological purity! The dialectic of the master and the slave. The class struggle.

Does blood imply life? Will hope spring eternal at the sight of it? In the spectators as well as the actors? What's the difference between our commitment and a bloody old melodrama? *Laureolus* held the stage for two centuries in Rome by the beauty of its ending: the crucified brigand was flung to a wild bear. And we: starting from other truths, we are renewing the assassinations and persecutions that built the Church. What torments me is the love that must inspire this necessary violence.

Once at the Academy of Venice, I stood for some time before Gentile Bellini's *Procession of the Relics*. "What's so unusual about it?" asked a Dutch colleague, Piet van Steel.

"It's a Bellini and it speaks to me of the proletariat," I said, "the revolution." Did that shock him? I don't know. Crazy as it sounds, I was telling the truth. I don't know why that blatantly lugubrious procession across the piazza should symbolize a classless society for me.

I was a young student and had plunged into Marxist literature with a beginner's fervor. Marx was fashionable just then. The Parisian Jesuits in Action Populaire had led the way. I honestly believed that I was following in the footsteps of Father Chambre and Father Calvez. Even in Rome, men like the German Wetter had for some time been responding to Marxism with other than the customary insults. I was full of zeal, persuaded that the problem would arise one day in my own country. When I returned from Italy I appalled my Flemish colleagues. For them philosophy, like theology, ran along the royal road of Saint Thomas. Of course they vaguely wanted peace and material prosperity for my compatriots. But it was left to the Church's specialists in Social Doctrine to light their path. Pius XI and Leo

XIII were the only certain guides. On Marx, Lenin, the revolution, and other disastrous myths, they contented themselves with authority and revelation, which they passed along to their students.

A comedy or a tragedy? I found it painful at first, but soon grew accustomed to it. Especially to that wonderful concept, "spiritual poverty." So agreeable. Now and then I worried: a compromise between faith and temporal power could in no way advance justice. I learned quickly to accept reality—even if I felt occasionally that despite myself, but because of my faith, I would always land on the side of institutionalized injustice. That was why I wanted to break with them.

He's still prating. It will soon be nine o'clock. The prospect of deliverance helps me feign attention for another few minutes. Under my breath I try a prayer, a psalm, an Hour of the breviary. The immediate problem is to keep my dry barren heart human. The everyday language of life, of lectures, of religion, is no longer, not for years now, much more than a flow of sounds and images appropriate to certain worlds. Didn't I enjoy them for long years in my desire to conform, and even love them in a purely aesthetic sense? Was my spiritual intoxication only a matter of conditioned reflexes? Since I began reciting the Hours in French the words are more stylish and eloquent but the sentiment moves me less. Day before yesterday I was reciting Prime during a class, and I was struck by a shallow figure of speech, and I smiled. The professor was in full flight, demonstrating that Christianity was the handmaiden of capitalism, and he glowered ferociously at me. He's like me in that: smiles and glances upset him.

What do I pray for now but the desire to share fully in my comrades' dream? To join them in action, and in their sick thinking—sick because it's overly schematic and it's all the doctrine they have. I want us to be the midwives of a healthier society, so the sacrifice on the Cross will no longer be a lie. But how far can I stray from myself? No. Hold down the rising panic. If there's no one I can share this anguish with, too bad.

Sanguinetti used to talk about the transcendant state of priestly solitude. In his mouth it was a well-turned phrase, the kind he liked. Now I try to comprehend it, to feel its proper weight of meaning. André Nsansi, once of my parish, is in camp; he avoids me carefully. When I first saw him I approached him, hand outstretched, my heart rising; he looked me in the eye and spat. He did not understand me. What is it in me that he scorns? The priest or the new militant? There he is in the first row, drinking in the new gospel. If only I were all of a piece like him! In my hatred as in my love.

I've accepted my solitude and admitted my eternal damnation, but I'll never learn to live with ostracism. Why should I be a bastard? I'm one of them; I want to become what they are, heart and soul. Why do they greet me with contempt? Why do they reject me—the sudden heavy silence when I join a group lively until my approach; curious and even homicidal glances; unintelligible muttering as I pass by? What have I done? Am I forever damned? And yet—is not my dream, with all its promise, the same as theirs?

2

AMAZING THAT I'M RECONCILED to my own body. Exhaustion tells me to cherish it, as one might cherish a notably unlucky man. Stretched on my wooden bunk, I say hello to my *nkusu* and wallow in the luxury of the free half hour before the noonday meal. Physical training drains me, and I drop onto my bed, a dead soul. These moments of truce—what happiness! But it would be dangerous to linger over fleeting reprieves. I defy my conscience only for the moment. My balance lies in pushing toward the truth, in efforts to break through the earthbound opacity of scholastic theology. Unrestrained melancholy would be just as dangerous. Another clerical vice: hot-eyed, factitiously maintained metaphysical agonies. I already have a penchant for that sort of self-indulgence. The disembodied sorrow on the face of Botticelli's *Venus*, with whom I fell in love at the Uffizi in Florence, is an essentially Christian melancholy: abstract interrogations unrelated to everyday life. One shrinks from them. I wasted a lot of time over those sterile, luxurious problems. My doctoral thesis is a scandalous proof:

"Echoes of Platonism in the Thought of Marius Victorinus."
Today my mission is to deny, by my very presence, God's responsibility in colonialism, as in exploitation. The primary obstacle is myself, with my pious, mechanical, obligatory phrases,
my European education, and my respectable manner. I reek of a
tradition. You can even see it in my stride. I have wandered too
far. Yes, and in what direction?

"You will betray," said my Superior when I told him my plans.
    "Betray whom?"
    "Christ."
    "Not Europe, Father? And is it really treason? Haven't I the
right to divorce a Christianity that has betrayed the Gospel?"
    "You're a priest, Pierre."
    "Forgive me, Father: I am a black priest."
    Father Howard had shut his eyes and bowed his head
abruptly, as if overcome by a sudden attack. A few moments later
he raised a tense face. His large brown eyes bored into me. I
thought, his is the self-confidence of the lords of the earth. Of a
race not mine—the race of empire-builders. It is men like him
who boast of Bernanos to enhance the Church's prestige. All he
meant to me now was that stare. Was he judging me? At that
moment I was no more to him than a tool that no longer works
properly. They will reject me. I have broken something. He rose;
he paced his office. For the first time I did not laugh at the sort
of man who can only think straight walking back and forth.
    "No, my son," Father Howard went on, "that would be a
crime. I tell you: a crime. A very grave dereliction. Of yourself
most of all. You cannot descend to it. Your spiritual state forbids
you. And how useless it would be! Look at history. How many
crises the Church has undergone! How many failures of nerve!
How many churchmen have chosen precisely the wrong moment
to meddle in secular brawls! And what good did it do anyone?
What cause did it further? Tell me."
    Here I found my Superior amusing. All I wanted was to

forestall an incipient headache. I contemplated the garden scorched by a pitiless sun. Plants dozed, leaves dangled. Would my spiritual state bar me from joining those who create or transform the world? In a sudden illumination I sensed the truth in those exalted Christians of the Italian sixteenth century, those misunderstood monsters so full of love, the Savonarolas, the Braccio de Montones. . . . The insanity of a motto: *Jesus Christus Rex populi Florentini S.P.Q. decreto creatus.* That's dreadful. But not so different from the Virgin Mary, generalissima of the armies in the Spanish twentieth century. So the Church would condone secular action only under certain conditions. . . . Let the good Father rattle on—what brawls do not involve the Church? At the seminary they stuffed our heads with Pontifical Documents. A whole encyclopedia. A true Catholic line on anything and everything: football and the movies, bike races and international politics, the latest scientific discoveries and philological extrapolations from Cicero's Latin or Heidegger's aesthetic . . .

"Pierre, Pierre." He spoke lower; I paid heed. "I know you. I have confidence in your intelligence, and even more in your faith. Don't let yourself be carried away by slogans. You know your duty: to stay here, in the service of all." He held out the open packet: "Take a cigarette."

I accepted one, set it between my lips, and bent toward his lighter. My hands trembled. That panic again, betraying me every time . . .

Howard spoke softly: "As priests we have no right to enlist on one side or another. We must resist the seductions of vengeance even when they seem the seductions of justice. That is the cross we bear . . . our temptation, Pierre. Our crucifixion."

"That's all talk, Father, and you know it."

He pulled up sharply. My violence had taken him by surprise. Encouraged by my own audacity, I rushed on: "Life is like the Gospel. He who is not with me is against me. In this country the Church has its head in the clouds, but its feet in the mud.

Her interests have never been God's. In the past, at least—I
grant you that. Father Superior, you preach that God is an end.
So do I. But all about us God is only a means. We priests close
our eyes to that. You know perfectly well why; better than I, no
doubt."

I stopped there, breathless after my sudden outburst. The
words had come to me as if I were being prompted. I feared
suddenly that I had been unfair. Could I make it up to him? No.
Too late. Father Howard gazed sadly at me. A spasm of pain
flashed through my back. I noticed the heat, and opened the
topmost button of my cassock. This is what Hell is like, I decided. Not to be sure of anything, to be in the grip of an animal
fear that freezes your belly, to be scorched by your own anguish.
Well, think of something else. No. Why ignore this? I can't
ignore being a priest. That's a certainty. And Father Howard is
a priest like me. There's the tie that binds us. Is it the only one?
No. We have much in common.

Classical music. Vivaldi, Mozart, Bach. For two years we
spent long evenings together in a kind of conspiracy, enjoying
but never avowing a common vice. Dinner cleared away, we sat
on the terrace, looking out over the garden. The cool evening
air. The brooding night. A glass of whiskey. And music rising,
sweet, intoxicating, voluptuous . . . a kind of sacrament. Sometimes he chose the records, sometimes I did. It was apparently a
random selection—but why then this sense of continuity, of
orderly progress evening after evening? I never felt any special
preference, any wish for this or that record. He and I were
enough alike so that each evening prolonged the imperishable
pleasures of the previous evening. For him as for me. Time
passed. . . . Those were perhaps the only hours of happiness, of
immediate beauty, that I have ever experienced without an inner
clash.

And then the books we loved. We passed them back and
forth. Our common memories of Rome. Our impassioned debates on the role of the priest, like our debates on literature and

the detective novels we both devoured. I'm closer to Father
Howard than I am to my own countrymen—even to the priests
among them.

One thing only separates us: the color of our skin. And why
does that matter? I know it does not matter. It begins to matter
only when analogies unbalance the argument. Howard's compatriots and my own. Masters and serfs. Christianity: their religion.
I must have betrayed my origins spontaneously and ingenuously
to feel so comfortable in a system that my grandfather had never
heard of. They imported their faith with the rest. My father
believed, had himself baptized, had me baptized. Why? Was any
alternative open to him? Particularly under colonialism, where
Christianity justified political power and political power in turn
imposed the faith? Could one survive without yielding, accept-
ing the master's religion? My parents accepted it; made me accept it; and I have been a priest for ten years. A priest in a foreign
religion.

If only I had been lucky enough to suffer forced baptism!
The whole matter would be so simple. My self-contradictions
would not exist. Or would be far weaker. Or say, less active. And
yet I thought I had rid myself of these tensions. And suddenly
things fell apart because I wanted to live as Jesus Christ's priest.

Father Howard appealed to me: "Pierre."

I looked him in the eye. Was it only pretended sadness that
I read? Doubt entered my soul. Why, God? Why? Can Howard
be right?

"Pierre," he said again, "the Church can be wrong in its
servants. It consists of men like you and me. I understand your
temptation. But error and abuses exist wherever man exists. You
know that: your brother is a politician."

His words struck home. Hard. The implication was clear.
He was referring to a recent indelicacy on my brother's part that
had cost him a few months in prison. My scruples vanished.
"But, Father—"

"It's no use to go on arguing," he said. "You're bound by

your vow of obedience. Bear that in mind. I act for the Bishop here and I deny your right to leave the parish on the pretext of helping our people among the guerrillas. You're an authority on canon law. I need say no more."

He lit a cigarette for himself, and I noticed that for the first time in the two years I had lived with him he omitted the courtesy of offering me one. Distracted, no doubt. He resumed: "Remember a sentence you must recognize: *Domine, imposuisti homines super capita nostra et bene fecisti* (Lord, you have placed some people above us and you have done well). Be humble, Pierre, and admit that no one is indispensable, not even you. I'll talk it over with the Bishop. Courage, Pierre: I'll pray for you."

He was dismissing me. I rose; I left; I felt his gaze on the back of my head. The rest followed as if in an extremely rapid dream. The harness fell away, just like that. And just like that, with a certain astonishment, I no longer felt the bit tugging at my mouth. Was I free? What is that, to be free? No more whip, no more bridle, or no more nose bag? No second thoughts. I headed for the lavatory; my bowel clamored. The act restored my peace of mind. At my door I ripped away my visiting card and glanced at it. Handsome print: for the first time I realized how handsome. My brother had made me a gift of a thousand of them when I was nominated vicar of Kosolo. The handsome letters commenced dancing before my eyes. Pierre Landu, Vicar, Pierre Vicar Landu, Landu Vicar Pierre. Vicar Pierre Landu . . . amusing. Was my dream of selflessness to end in a game?

Once in my room I slipped off my cassock, and set my breviary beside my rosary at the center of my worktable. I knelt. My mind was empty; an intolerable calm. I was alone, prisoner of my contradictions. I crossed myself. A mechanical act or a magic rite? It hardly mattered. I needed the symbol. A sign of the cross to end the tormented complacency of the petit bourgeois I had become, and to start the adventures of the witness that I wished in the end to become.

And I left for the jungle, after slipping this letter into Father Howard's mailbox:

Please be kind enough, Father Superior, to advise Monsignor the Bishop that I have left to join the guerrillas. I am not renouncing my priesthood, nor leaving the Church. I want to join others in creating a new world, where our Lord Jesus will no longer be disfigured. He consoles us in our afflictions so that we may console the afflicted by living among them. I can no longer hesitate. To remain here in the parish would be to betray my conscience as an African and a priest. I choose sword and fire so that, in a new world, my people will recognize Him as their own.
      Pray for me.
                                    Pierre Landu, *priest*

Now a sharp tapping echoes through my drowse. Some danger? No; it's Antoinette, my nearest neighbor. I remember my shock the first day: a mixed barracks!

"Don't worry about it, big man," Bidoule told me in his husky voice. "The rules are strict. You'll be assigned specific hours for rest."

The first night was terrible. The day's exhausting exercises had promised sleep. But all those dark bodies twisting casually in the gloom were most intriguing. I am too weak. The creaking and crackling of the bunks had ended my nights of virtuous dreams. Wasn't it the same creaking and crackling I'd heard in my aunt's house, when I was a child and spent my vacations with her? Irregular whispers, punctuated by sighs. And then much later, the troubling silence that drew me down into a sleep where my aunt and innumerable cousins, heads shaved, performed the dance of the Word.

But no; these here had gone peacefully off to sleep. Following orders. And yet the hook had sunk deep; was I the only one? What does a sleeping woman smell like? Stupid. For more than twenty years that same question had made my nights poignant.

Antoinette. I noticed suddenly that she was sitting up on her bunk, facing mine, with a weary smile for me. Her eyes—yes, the crinkles, the crinkles at the corners of her eyes lent her that look of—what? Eyes beloved and revered by God. Where had I read that phrase?

"So, Pierre." A quick forced laugh. Why should she laugh? She's spoiled everything. "You won't last long if you go on like this."

"Yes, I will."

"Will you? With me . . . no. You wouldn't understand." Her hands gestured vaguely. The swell of her bosom, her long arms in the light sweater; yes, hers was the throbbing life of glorious poverty.

Was she immune to this heat?

"I'd understand. I'm a priest. You all know that, don't you?"

"Then why are you here?"

Again that implicit verdict. Always the same. Should I explain? Obviously; the fact demands a reason, the effect demands a cause. Ah, what would Sanguinetti have done in my place? I sat up on my bunk and faced her directly.

"Pierre, do you know what the others are doing? No? They're just making love. Is that foolish? No, it's relaxing. But a little tiring at this time."

Making love. The old phrase. As if there were anyone on earth capable of inventing love.

She glanced away. The instinct was sound. The attraction of the cold lonely peaks of purity. "You condemn me, don't you?"

"Of course I don't condemn you. Not at all. Believe me. But love is quite demanding."

"Yes. It is. Why are you here?" A bitter smile this time; languid lids hid her sad eyes.

"For the same reason as you, I imagine."

"You're wrong. They brought me in by force. Like most of the women here."

"Ah!"

She smiled. The fold of her eyelids: those crinkles again. Those will enslave me for good. Slavery, I decided, was adoration.

"You haven't answered."

I melted. Were her eyes stripping me naked? What a child I was suddenly!

The foolishness of innocence. So much the better. "Do you want me to say that I believe in the revolution?"

Would she never stop smiling! Any anger, any violence, dies away.

Shall I tell her that here I can live without divorcing theory from practice? Shall I confide in her? Admit that I am hoping to break strong habits formed by my special background, by the theoretical bases of a clerical education? Those clear eyes. What sort of woman will she be in two years? I'd love to follow her. To watch her glide through time. What will she look like in ten years?

"You're a perfectionist, Pierre."

"No, come on now. I want to join the struggle for justice. God exists. I love mankind, the quick and the dead, but mainly the quick, the living, mankind today. You and the others. We're fighting for a better world. A revolution. Listen: a Christian ought to be in a permanent state of revolution. I just want to be a Christian."

Only words? Her open face expressed a more important truth. How could I presume to preach? I was ashamed of my fine phrases and the gust of religiosity rising within me. How could I explain? I tried: "Antoinette, I'm here because I can't come to terms anymore with a history that stupidly compromised Christ and that, unfortunately, many members of my Church still stand for. Most of them, in this country. If I stay with them, fit into their organizations and institutions, I betray. And how can I live in peace except with people who really *work*, by action, for the triumph of justice? I claim Christ for my guide. He was a revo-

lutionary! The nice people thought so. That's why they crucified
Him. As a priest, I was answerable to Him."

Did she understand me? Should I have expected a reaction?
Another temptation: this need to be understood, to be approved.
A slave mentality. I needed her. I was using her to find peace.
An actor, I told myself. A clown? Impossible. Her silence: What
was she thinking of? I hardly dared move. Dispossessed. A sac-
rilegious gleam stung my eyes.

. . . Hold forth a hand. Harvest a fruit, share my suffering
in the rejection of a mythic mystery.

"Do you think my ideals are only my eccentricity exagger-
ated?"

"What does that mean? I don't understand you."

There we are: I was too complicated. The idiot mark of a
university career. At Koloso, Father Howard read through all my
sermons, charitably helping me simplify them. But isn't simplification sometimes impoverishment? How to convey the richness
of the message with a poverty of symbols? If we oversimplify the
form, don't we kill the content? If we purify it of life's eddies and
agitations, doesn't it become a sensational blurb, no longer true
because all the human shades and subtleties have been wrung out
of it? If I failed to make myself understood, or if I digressed,
would it prove that my culture, like my Christianity, is only a
superficial husk around my black kernel?

She was gazing at me, lost and helpless.

"Antoinette—what I mean is—if you think that—"

A strident shout tore through my memory. Rome. Via
Veneto. A fire truck runs down a woman. A scream. It's the
same cry for help. Blood. My throat dries. . . . My mouth fell
open; I was thirsty. Antoinette: eyes like a sleepy pond in the
shadow of long grasses. The silence was heavy with an immea-
surable longing for human communion. A warm dream unfolded
before my eyes. It is the Voice. In Malle's *Les Amants* . . . no.
Jeanne Tournier did not attend polo matches at Bagatelle because she loved the game. She did not come for pleasure or out

of snobbery. She even felt lost among the crowd. She came
because Raoul Flores was her lover. That was nothing; it was
normal; but for her it was enormous, because it was "her first."
The Voice. That voice. And the other, in the Via Veneto . . .
And Maggy: "Jeanne, look at me; please look at me." Jeanne's
smile as she lay dying. The crinkles in Antoinette's eyelids.
Finally a sad pluck at my shoulder; a wounded bird's cry. A sting
amid the flow of saliva on my trembling tongue. And those full
lips, abandoned. If they could only resume life in all the glory of
the flesh.

O hunger. That hand: if I could clasp it with my own. Press
it, break down the walls. Only once . . . *Les Amants*: the luxurious bathroom, eyes meeting in the mirror, adoration:

> Bernard: Tell me that—
> Jeanne: I love you.
> Bernard: Forever?
> Jeanne: Forever.

For all eternity. That affliction of the heart. And the singing look, the smile in the eyes; tears; flashes of sunlight. Bernard:
"Let's run away, just leave, the two of us together. I feel like
killing off the whole rest of the world. That would be more
polite." Jeanne's room. My hand on her wrist. No, that's Bernard. Is he me?

Antoinette: I offered my hand. To live out my transfiguration at last. An inner *click!*, an automatic reaction: my hands disgusted me. A futile fling: I felt a violent contempt for my own
flesh. Strictly conditioned, I thought. That is "actual grace." A
smile must have softened my face; Antoinette responded. Perhaps
she had divined my frailty. It was all over. I was once more a block
of ice, predestined to chastity. Nevertheless, I touched her hand.
I heard myself murmur, "God is good." And reproached myself for
managing no better thanks than that gambit.

"Which God?" She confided in me: "I believe in God, but
Catholicism is a religion for white people."

"That's not true."

"It is, it is! How is it better than my ancestors' religion? You're duty-bound to defend it, even if that's treason here. You're not really one of us. But why should I accept it? Bidoule says we're free people in a country that claims to be free. So I can't be a slave to the whites any more."

"My poor Antoinette, I understand."

"No. I don't need your pity. Why do you say 'poor'? I'm not poor. You Catholics are all the same. Always that superior attitude, so you pity anything not Catholic. Are you really black, Pierre?"

I knew about that. I understood her better than she believed. What obliged her to put her faith in a foreign religion? Catholic, universal, what you will, the problem remains: Catholicism springs from the Western world. Even to understand it is European. It is supported by Europe's institutions, and one can love it only by enrolling oneself in the history of a civilization. Again I see Sanguinetti's color slides. The Mass meant to commemorate the Last Supper was worship of the feudal emperor. The Last Supper immortalized by da Vinci. As Ghirlandaio offered *The Visitation;* da Fabriano, *The Adoration of the Magi;* Verocchio, *The Baptism of Jesus;* Mantegna, *The Dead Christ;* Giotto and Fra Angelico, *The Deposition;* Bellini, *The Resurrection of Jesus;* Signorelli, *The Resurrection of the Flesh.* The grace of Venuses and Madonnas, of Apollos and Jesuses, is all the same. I am at home with it. The Scriptures have melted into human flesh, marked by the colors and highlights of a civilization that has become mine. The ingenious—and genius's—alchemy of one History and one Religion. Has that fusion really failed?

So: I see no convincing way to persuade an African to opt for Catholicism, other than conditioned reflexes. Since early childhood I have lived in the Citadel. Now doubt gnaws at me, precisely because I'm trying, by the life I live, to isolate the essence of the myths. "Antoinette—if you don't mind, I want to rest now. You're probably right."

I lay back. I had been cowardly. It was all over. Now she knew. A priest had solicited her. I was that priest. To forget my own anguish! Now my whole being is only a desperate offering to moral suicide. Pray: I must pray. "Pierre, lovest thou Me?" "Yes, Lord; Thou knowest that I love Thee." And yet I denied Him. But was it He whom I denied? I grew drowsy. In the haze I heard Antoinette stretch out upon her bed. I abandoned myself to the *nkusu*. The empty desert of sleep and unconsciousness. Finally to live happily, for a few hours.

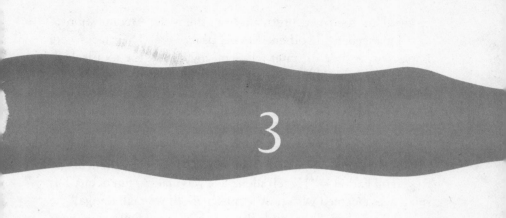

3

SHOUTS, A CLAMOR. THIS IS MY life. My undarned socks bring home my happiness. I have never so seriously pondered the utility of socks: what a superfluous restraint! I slip into the din of living creatures. The dormitory is like a chicken coop at feeding time. Outside, rain falls in dense sheets. We had to break off the calisthenics. A revised schedule. We're waiting for orders. And in the heat of my comrades' uproar, I hope for the amnesia that will put an end to my past.

Bidoule has come in, flanked by Garbage Girl, his factotum. A circle gathered. Naturally enough. The call of real life. Hunched over a map, Bidoule spoke. He was handsome in profile, with his broad, sloping chest. "Right there is Kanga. Yesterday it was occupied by troops sent up from Charlesville. We're going to wipe them out; we leave in fifteen minutes. All groups by truck to within five kilometers of the garrison. On foot from there. There's no danger south of the village. You see it now? Kanga, there on the right bank of the river. Lion group attacks from the northeast. Jackal from the north. Serpent attacks directly along the river, upstream from the west. Any questions?"

I glanced at the others. My baptism of fire. Their faces were impassive. A drop of water fell upon my cheek; the roof leaked. The rain would double our misery. A crazy idea—this maiden attack, in a downpour! I'd come out of it with at least a bad cold.

"I remind you of your orders. We're attacking the troops and only the troops. But shoot down any armed man. We leave in fifteen minutes. Be ready. Pierre Landu, follow me."

He led me out of the barracks. "If we take the village, Reverend Father—" He fell silent. He was making fun of me. His small eyes gleamed with hostile mischief. "If we take Kanga," he began again, "you'll head for the parish church. Follow Garbage Girl's group. There'll be five or six of you. You can buy stores there and meet us at the northern village gate."

"Buy stores?" I didn't understand. Not at all. He guessed it.

"Of course. *We* don't loot. We buy. Sometimes we put a little pressure on the seller. But we buy. That's not what the Charlesville newspapers say, but that's how it is."

In the truck carrying me to my second baptism I tried to clear my head. An absurd choice. Why me? They wanted me to corrupt myself beyond redemption in the sight of my fellow Catholics. Which priests served the Kanga parish? Well, it's better this way. Maybe. Except that I have never denied my calling, never unfrocked myself. The truck jounced forward with an effort; rain was still lashing down. All I could think of was Kanga. I saw myself confronting my colleagues, demanding their foodstuffs, ready to fire at the slightest resistance from any of them. A strict order to myself: keep calm. Teaching oneself how to die—is that silence the ultimate answer to the craving for a full life?

Suddenly I felt rotten, dizzy, as if swept down by an undertow. I thought: I've wandered from the path. The whole point is to go all the way. I can die later.

The truck halted. Rain was still pouring down. The heavens raged. To attack in weather like that was almost cowardly. And

in the event, Kanga was quickly reduced. The soldiery surren-
dered without a fight. We marched into the village singing. A
carefree afternoon? I had surprised myself in a moment of happiness and was amazed at my gaiety, on that road swamped by
rain. It was a real rogue's march. It filled me with joy. The poor
man's revenge, the dispossessed defending their own happiness
in good order, obsessed and half mad!

Bidoule had deployed the troops in three columns. How
many—three hundred? Five hundred? Two submachine guns had
opened fire. Hardly three seconds. Neat work, very neat. A bit
depressing, but absolutely by the book. Angry at myself, I tried
to subdue the *Magnificat* swelling in my heart. I told myself, you
must not rejoice! Why not? Soldiers were surrendering, others
were trying to escape. Bullets cropped both kinds. Bidoule's logic
was elementary: What would we do with prisoners? Especially
brutes like these? The sincerity and brutality of the proceedings
shadowed my good cheer. I took refuge in pure reason. At least
reason knows neither holiness nor ecstasy before a massacre.
Reason would sometimes justify an action, but could never simplify it to this point.

Does truth require reason? May tolerance and delicacy be
only weaknesses, when one is defending the truth? Sanguinetti:
"Truth suffers neither hesitation nor distortion. The light is always the light." The Inquisition had not defended a specific
order but Order and Truth. "The greatness of the Church is that
she has men who will do what must be done." The demands of
truth. These notions consoled me and troubled me. Was I fit to
uphold such arguments? I felt like vomiting. My body was pro-
testing. Far off I heard Bidoule's voice: "On the double, Pierre—
to the church."

I rushed forward. Two men. Garbage Girl. Those were my
orders: three or four. There were four of us. I halted abruptly and
turned to Garbage Girl: "But I have no money."

"I have it," she answered dryly.

I was about to step out again when I saw a soldier on my

right. He was crawling and covered with blood. I stepped closer.
This taste for the macabre was a perfectly priestly urge. Strong
feelings mingled, an apostolic fire and an ardent charity. Or so I
thought. I dropped to one knee. He stared at me, trembling,
hollow-eyed, jaw muscles contracted; his right elbow might have
been driven into the mud, and his left hand trembled on his
bloodsoaked chest. He believed I was about to kill him. I leaned
over him. "I am a priest."

He murmured something I could not understand. I leaned
closer, raised his chin and repeated, "I am a priest."

He was still staring amazed at me. Gone mad or stupefied,
no doubt. Suddenly he opened his mouth and spat in my face.

"Fool!" I hardly had time to regret my stupid insult; behind
me Garbage Girl shouted, "Finish him off!"

I contemplated the dying man. His eyes were immensely
wide, his mouth was stretched open to the rain. Wiping away
spittle, I turned back to Garbage Girl. She watched me scorn-
fully. I was ashamed of myself.

"Finish him off."

"Look at him! He's dead."

"I said, finish him off. That's an order."

My cup was full. To go all-out over a corpse. I was in an
unimaginable funk, scared to death. I knew this whole idiotic
scene would be reported in detail to Bidoule. Maybe even to the
Colonel. A real test of my good faith. I questioned my comrades
with a glance. They stood like statues, in a semicircle. Garbage
Girl's eyes were utterly discouraging: holy innocence and supreme scorn. I was diminished; nothing; so small, so contemptible in the fear that sweated from me. A ray of light: a sentence
from Ignatius Loyola flashed through my mind: Before acting,
pray; then act as if God did not exist. It was all linked, it
followed. Scripture came to the rescue: The ways of God are
unfathomable. Even unto the highest. *Usque ad summum.* I took
up my rifle, aimed, both eyes open, and shot him in the face.

"Well done, Priest. Now to church."

She might at least have added a short speech of congratulation. I listened uneasily to my heart: Would it stop? It beat on. A step up for me. I glided, serene. Not for anything in the world would I have missed the peace that suffused me at that moment.

No, no; it was important. Why should I doubt my own commitment now? Doubtless I do not understand what my position demands. The most capricious shifts of my heart become extraordinary events to me, marring all my joy. The clatter of a truck, blasting through the forest at insane speeds, reverberated throughout my body. Exhausted? This was exhaustion. Mainly physical. Morally my peaceful vigor was scandalous. Sadly peaceful, I confess. A dance of the devil sang at me from my early childhood:

> Ah, the sadness! Ah, the suffering!
> What sadness, what suffering!
> The sadness will kill me! Ah, what sadness!
> Ah, what suffering! What sadness, what suffering!

Yes, the sadness of being a priest. The priest that I am, with this passion for taking personal responsibility whenever God is about. Only to make my country human: just human. And isn't this raid by comrades a necessary clarification? I am now convinced: the Catholic hierarchy's detestation of all nationalist movements is based in part on a clear desire to safeguard, at any cost, the unjust privileges inherited from colonialism. And sometimes, as with the brave priest at Kanga, that leads to a false equation of religion with social standing. But doesn't the growth of Christianity in this country depend on a return to sources, to fundamentals purified of all the myths that cling to history? And I believe that only the extreme left can help us to conserve the essential and at the same time permit the Church to abolish the shameful compromises that still bind it to capitalist economy.

Absolutely ridiculous, that scene at the rectory in Kanga. How can anyone deny the Gospels to that point? I grant you the

inevitable bourgeois influence on foreign missionaries. I lived
under it for years and found myself extremely comfortable with
it. But that influence is no more necessary to the propagation of
the faith than material wealth is to the transcendence of Christianity. It's really the other way around. In any case, the Gospels
are categorical.

"I cannot give you anything," he had said. "These goods
belong to the Christian community of Kanga."

Only a voice. False humility. If that is the voice of a martyr,
Lord, preserve me from martyrdom. I fail to see how it glorifies
You.

"These goods," he went on, "seem to you abundant, ex-
travagant. Yet they are necessary to the completion of the ministry of love we have taken upon ourselves. Besides"—an
insistent smile—"the Church is not a commercial establish-
ment."

Garbage Girl put an end to the painful playacting with
mockery that threw sparks: "Then if you refuse to sell us stores,
Father, you will surely not refuse to share them with us in Christian charity?" And wickedly added, "I feel sure that Father
Landu, who is one of us"—and she gestured toward me—"will
give us absolution for the sin, if it is one."

She marched out of the room in a burst of laughter. The
parish priest stood wide-eyed. He stared at me, shocked. A crazy
urge to laugh rose in me. This time I've had it, I told myself: I'll
be suspended. So much the worse. My colleague's stupidity confirmed my new loyalty. In the truck taking me back to camp I
meditated the need to cleanse the Temple. The money changers
have swarmed in again. What a sanctimonious horror! They
preach charity and generosity to the poorest of God's creatures
and rob them, with a clear conscience, of the little they possess.
Not all priests, of course; but we all share the profits. In my
country the Church was a band of international brigands doing
their dirty work under the sign of God. Knowingly or unknow-
ingly they were thieves, and that included me too. Those 1,250

acres of parish land in Kanga, cultivated by the catechumens! And all they're entitled to in return, these chosen of God, is one skimpy meal a day and two hours of religious instruction. The work of communion and the message of charity have become alibis for commercial enterprises. Neither faith nor the religious life any longer serves purely human purposes. Bad faith and bad conscience have been stretched to the limit.

Tired. I forced myself to stop thinking about it, to relax, let myself go. To become a thing, a sack of tripes. Taking revenge on the executioner that is my spirit.

I wanted to think about God, but I felt only the weight of my fatigue. A brutal sense of absence invaded me. A void.

"What's the trouble, Comrade?" asked my neighbor.

I must have spoken aloud. What did I say? That despairing sense of absence transfixed me.

"Nothing. God has fled."

Laughter answered me. I slump in my seat, and my eyes search the void. I'm drunk on this new pain. Nothing exists now but my purpose and my pain. But I feel a frightful need of God. Is this all-pervasive absence a sign of love? It cannot be a simple negation; not possibly. Only that void justifies my purpose, my life. I believe. I continue to believe precisely because He is no longer present to me. His absence is yet a presence. His passion. His power to forgive may yet reveal itself. Thorns, lashes. My God and my Master . . . That was not true. I was happier re-calling Aldo Palazzeschi. The poetic flow of lyrics and gestures. The airy beat came back to me. I choked up, and swayed to the verses:

> Le piccole chiese al crepusculo s'aprono
> ne sortono lente le suore ed enfilano il ponte
> nel mezzo s'incrocian, s'inchinan
> le bianche e le nere
> si recan l'un valtre ella piccola chiesa al saluto
> vi fanno una breve preghiera

e leste rinfilano il ponte.
Di nuovo s'incontran, s'inchinan le file, una biancha e
    una nera,
le suore s'incrocian la sera
la sera al crepusculo..

[The small churches open at dusk
The nuns come out slowly and walk through
    the bridge
They meet in the middle, salute each other
Those in white and those in black
They advance, all of them, towards the chapel
    for the service
They make a brief prayer
Then slowly they walk again through the bridge
And again their lines meet
And they salute each other
The one in white and the one in black
The nuns meet in the evening
In the evening at dusk.]

The brilliant passage was close to sacrilege. In my present
place, so was I. I was in agony; my mind clutched at psalms. To
sift out the meaning and learn the words again. God would
come. My spirit would open.

Veni Creator Spiritus . . . Naked, unpretentious, and not
mocking, the verses answered the truck's jolts, and finally I could
hope that my exhaustion was not without purpose.

Slowly a great fervor swelled in me, filling my emptiness the
moment I set foot in this hut. I even crossed myself sketchily, out
of habit, as I do when I enter even the smallest church. This was
no church, but an armory. My instinctive ritual was a response
to the calm and silence that fell upon me as I crossed the thresh-
old. This was my first moment alone since my arrival. Why had
Bidoule chosen me? Never mind; I was there and alone, and that
was a blessing. Ostensibly to stack and count the arms retaken

from the government forces. The solitude reminded me of those luxurious hours of silence that a priest usually devotes to God.

It was almost time. Rome, once again. Afternoon classes bored me. And in the overheated classroom—they all are, at the Angelicum in winter—I awaited impatiently the bell that would announce the hour of meditation. A bath of peace that would calm my soul, in the humid sweet church, that would wash away the day's cares. A true respite. Was that small reward for a day's work so different from the annual vacation? Wasn't the long holiday also a kind of revenge on the year's work? It was a pause, as each day in late afternoon meditation slowed the hours. The orgy of peace and quiet I allowed myself every year in the Italian lake country had set me in a permanent attitude, a penchant not for piety but for the constant caress of a life without weariness.

Here I encountered the joys of solitude as a luxury, a masterpiece that a caring fate had reserved for me. A song I once heard crossed my mind: "The middle class is pigs. . . ." I couldn't remember the next line. But the truth of the phrase is embedded in me. Leisure—*there* is the great theft by today's upper classes. The days of "property is theft" are long gone. Now they need leisure to make up for life's purposeless little heroisms, or to forget them. When the black priest enlists, as I did, in a society organized to ration and allot hours of sleep and moments of laughter, hours of easy and pleasant reading and the eternity of painless studies, shouldn't he be willing to die for those of his people still striving and suffering to survive lives of menial service? Aren't meditations, like the canonical hours, really brief reprieves granted by an ever-expanding authority to maintain a small preserve of silence for those of its servants assigned to safeguard a way of life scarcely that of the Gospels?

There it is again: my prayer ends in a lugubrious disputation. The whoops and hollers and general indiscipline of young Roman ecclesiastics suddenly seemed quite funny. There too we had to respect the natural order of things and revealed truth:

youth unruly and unrulable. Even within the Church. She is not
of this world, but isn't she obliged to reflect it, even its illusions?
Sanguinetti used to talk about certain nocturnal rumpuses that
he disapproved of, but you could sense a singularly significant
leniency: "Yesterday four students came home at two in the
morning. That is inadmissible for seminarians. Even if they're
American." And indeed there was one American in the bunch.
He must have dragged the others along. Like a gang of school-
boys. That's curious, by the way—why do Americans, and even
American priests, seem so good-natured? We forgive them for
the most idiotic faux pas because there is so much candor in their
manner. Is it the influence of the Gospels or of leisure?

Prayer. A poem by Miguel Hernandez rose within me. Sorting,
tagging, counting submachine guns, light machine guns, and
rifles, I felt a surge of joy, brutally honest: it was my prayer for
this canonical hour. My offering:

> *Love, vaulting high*
> *Myself below, love*
> *Shining by the light of my own urges*
> *And no other*
> *Gaze upon me here, chained,*
> *Rejected, without warmth*
> *At the foot of the most sudden*
> *And ferocious gloom*
> *Eating bread and knife alike*
> *Like a good laborer,*
> *Sometimes only the knife*
> *And only for love.*

And only for love. That is what matters: love. How dreadful
that in the Church, where they talk constantly of love, where
God is love, there is no theology of love, just as there is no
theology of God. For twenty centuries the Church has clung to
History, adapting itself and its truths so as not to die of present

reality. Isn't my Church's whole theology a theology of contingencies?

That would be sad. For the moment, thank you, God, for even this oppressive silence, that spares me the sleep of contingencies.

4

"PIERRE LANDU! THE COLOnel's waiting for you!"

"He is, is he?" The merest twinge of anxiety. I am wallowing in indifference. Nothing surprises me now. When they called my name, all I felt was the duty to respond. And that not sharply. With my complicity confirmed, it is only partisan number 134, on permanent duty, who automatically rises. Why speculate? My present life is a provisionally definite response. I will simply give my colonel a true account of that life. Or perhaps justify some breach of discipline I may have committed.

Heavy-eyed, I go to meet Garbage Girl. She marches ahead of me at stiff parade. Frigid. Horribly confined by her masculine uniform. Why should they call her Garbage Girl? Any other woman in camp would more deserve the name.

Six-thirty. In an hour, full dark. I recall Father Howard, and his unwholesome comparisons: he established a curious link between the utter darkness of nights in the rainy season and the derriere of a black man hiding in a tunnel. Now that I can no

longer protest to him, my lips quiver in affection. At this very
moment he is reciting his breviary. In an hour he will go to
dinner; then to the terrace for a conversation with Mozart or
Vivaldi. My memory paints the scene in the colors of violent
temptation. The regular work, the healthy life, the tranquil career. I am brutally shamed by my slovenly trousers and my fancy
shirt oozing the sweat and grime of a week's manual labor.

Mosquitoes jab at my bare arms. I chase them with a few
loud slaps and then, annoyed by Garbage Girl's apparent immunity, let it go. But the bites, sharper than the *nkusu*'s, irritate
me. It seems unreasonable, losing face before this girl.

I know why I resent Garbage Girl: I cannot forgive her for
being different from the women I knew. She is isolated, hard,
self-sufficient, with an unalterable devotion to the demands of
the Revolution. The other women, brave peasant women from
my village, of my parish, all the women I greeted condescend-
ingly on the roads when I paraded my virtue murmuring prayers
during my late afternoon strolls—I knew myself for their master,
their pastor. Some were coy and secretive; I waited for them at
the bend of the road. "Hide it for now, my pretty: the day will
come when you will kneel at my feet and wash your dirty linen."
Father Howard was busy with accounts, bills, contracts, and
purchases to be made in town. I was the sole vicar, really, brother
of a fairly prominent politician: sooner or later, for one reason or
another, the whole village came to me. I was their master. Or,
to use a lovely ecclesiastical euphemism, I was their servant. A
powerful servant. And in this new setting, where all values are
reversed, this almost illiterate girl is my superior officer.

That last thought drew a hoarse exclamation from me. She
halted. A ragamuffin, I tell myself, only a ragamuffin!

"You spoke, Comrade?"

"Nothing. I was only wondering what was the feminine of
'colonel.'"

"The feminine of colonel," she said, "is colonel."

I felt foolish. Useless and foolish. I gritted my teeth; a curse swelled my cheeks. Garbage Girl cleared her own way through the grass, straight ahead. Reaching a path, she turned left. I tripped on a sort of furrow I hadn't seen. Immediately a dark figure took several steps toward us.

"The sun returns."

"The straw bleaches again," Garbage Girl answered.

"The driver is asleep."

"He is overcome by sleep."

"The rain will bring mud."

"The keys are hung on the stars."

"Advance," said the man, whom I could see clearly now.

Garbage Girl whispered a few words in his ear. The man inspected me, took me by the hand and tugged me closer, and raised the storm lantern to see my face. I was nervous. He stared at me for some seconds. "All right. Come on."

I followed him. He walked a few steps off the path. "Look here." His foot turned over a formless mass. "A corpse," he told me.

I leaned over it. He cast lantern light upon it.

It was a man, naked, still alive. A shallow breath barely stirred his chest. There was not much left of his face. His lips had been cut off; his nose too. Doubtless by a razor blade. Where his left eye had been there was only a hole. His forehead had been slashed and was lined with fresh dribbles of blood.

The sentry was beside me. Garbage Girl must have been standing behind us. I closed my eyes in disgust. My priesthood was shelter now: *Ego, te absolvo . . .* I recited in silence. These reaffirmations of the divine bond raised inner questions. I forgot the dying man and wondered if I had already—at that moment—been officially suspended by my bishop. He must have received the report from Kanga. I could imagine its tone. My lips tightened.

"You see," said the sentry. "Never try to come this way unless you've been sent for. The passwords change every day. Now follow me. The Colonel's waiting."

Almost immediately we were standing before a hut. Garbage Girl had disappeared. A sentry loomed out of the dark, demanded our numbers, then vanished into the night. Unlike our barracks, built on the lines of farm chapels, the Colonel's hut was like any peasant's hut in the region. Simplicity was here wedded to doctrine. In the luxury of our little chalets and our free time, we priests were caricatures of poverty. Our lives were not wedded to our message.

The sentry returned. "You may go in."

He was seated on a footstool with a book in his hand. A symbol. But I was nervous again, and recalled a photo in *Paris-Match* during the summer mutinies in 1960: a mutinous colonel sat in the same serious attitude. With a detective novel in his hand. Or maybe on his table, I couldn't remember exactly. Even symbols decayed. I glanced at the small storm lantern hung on the wall behind him. Impatiently I awaited the sound of his voice; for long seconds all I could see of him was his wide eyes. They bored into me. A moment of idiotic fellowship overwhelmed me.

"Good evening, Pierre. Getting used to us? Sit down. There, yes, take the stool. A cigarette?"

I accepted it. He had already overpowered me. Devotion flooded me. Through spirals of smoke I absorbed the affection in his eyes. I loved him. Violently.

"Now then, Pierre. How do you feel? Still excited?"

The word offended me and dejected me: he, too, was reducing my commitment to an impulse. I was disappointed, and told him so.

"Disappointed? But why? Ah—the simplicity of our methods? But that's our sort of purity, you see. Of act as of intent. And then, we're not intellectuals. A liberation movement is doomed once it stops to haggle over nuances of good and evil, once it starts to question its own goals. I know that's a humiliating state of affairs for an intellectual, and for the priestly soul most of all. Fine distinctions, adaptations of pardon and charity—that's your line of work. A line of work with its own rigid demands. Only it takes courage to admit that."

He smiled. That, I told myself, is a god's smile, of a universal generosity because it transcends time. He was dragging me into a warm greenhouse of humanity. As a chasm yawned at my feet, I took refuge in his eyes. Witchcraft. I tried to find a distraction, and stared brutishly at the book in his hand. He caught me up immediately.

"Spying on me already? The book is entitled *Moscow Calling*. An easy way to kill time, but a bit disappointing. By Nicholas Arjak. Would you care to borrow it? Ah, you know it? Right up to date, aren't you! But I was forgetting—these days Catholics study Marxism as much as Communists do. So anything anybody writes about Moscow or Marx sells pretty well. Where do I find these books? I swiped this one from a priest we sent to his heavenly rest. A real reactionary, that one. He'll be of more use where he is now. As a general rule I don't like to read. It tires one for no good reason. A few basic books will do the trick. . . . But you're a priest. I have a few books here you're bound to like. Wonderful rationalizations of wishful thinking; you'll find them consoling. *Le Royaume et ses exigences*, by Yves de Montcheuil. *La Découverte de Dieu* by Louis Mendigal—you've read them? I have others."

I was enthralled. The richest and most unexpected notions, stated in provocative euphemism, sounded pure and simple in his voice. My scruples fell away like old scales. I was no longer a traveler without baggage. Henceforth I would have, for viaticum, the memory of an approving smile.

"Did I keep you waiting long for this summons?"

"Yes," I said. "It depressed me." In his presence, my soul was naked and without mysteries.

"It was a necessary initiation." He smiled again. "The raid on Kanga—did it shake you up? Yes? I was expecting it would. That moment with the soldier you finished off was a revelation to us. You were stupid and cowardly—don't deny it, I won't believe you. We need cowards. Garbage men."

Heat rose to my face. A brief thinning of his lips worried

me. I swallowed salty saliva, and thought, "That's the taste of blood."

"Do you know Garbage Girl's story? Suzanne she was, who led you, and Bidoule brought her back from a raid. By force, naturally. That's Bidoule's way. He thinks a good sex life is as important to the men's morale as a balanced diet. Suzanne never let herself be taken. She fought off every comradely advance with one insult: 'Garbage!' And as rape is severely punished in camp, 'Garbage Girl' is the personification of virtue here. Funny, isn't it? For her, men are garbage. But she's a tough militant, and that's what counts."

He had a way of putting people at their ease. I was more than relaxed now, borne up by a euphoria that expunged all doubts and temptations. A blood knot, probably. Do men who kill for the same just cause come to share some ultimate serenity? I looked him over again. With his huge head, half bald, his peaceful eyes, an enormous chest straining against a short-sleeved shirt, he might have been an easygoing gym teacher on vacation.

"You're wondering what I am, I imagine. Well, I'm vicious and depraved. You heard me. I love good ganja, strong drink, and fat women. Yes, the fat ones. They're like round ripe fruit, tender and juicy. They bleed gold, Handsome boys too, it goes without saying. I am, as you say in your learned tongues—yes, thank you, polymorphous perverse. I also adore blood. It is a burning passion. I should have been a jungle beast. Do you see? I am, Pierre, a fundamentally immoral being. . . ."

He burst into laughter, which let me relax again. Immoral? Was he making fun of me? It was to justify his presence among the guerrillas. He deliberately expressed his judgments crudely, since in his case there was absolutely no moral norm, no system of reference. Yes, maybe Marxism. But I doubted that more and more.

"Yes, I'm only an anarchist, an activist who signs on to be an instrument and nothing more. A tool, a means. I'll settle for paving the way, even if I never see the promised land. I'm quite sure that some day I'll be shot in the back of the head. Most likely by a close comrade. I await that moment calmly; it will sanctify the brutishness of my life. A true moment of ecstasy, the promised orgasm."

His face shone. He seemed ethereally happy. I couldn't help thinking of the young Thérèse of Lisieux. It was the same passionate insistence: "I am a broom to be used and then put away again in a corner." The man offered himself as a simple instrument, to prepare a future he would never see. A priest or a poet.

I was dizzy; I felt myself sucked into his orbit. I was almost stupefied. "Here is a man with faith." The shares he bought with his blood were no comfortable blue chips. The once-oppressed colonial in him did not simply worship the negative. There was no self-hate, no derision of those he did hate. His hopes were modest. His dream was to be a small cog in the huge machine of this revolution.

"Tell me, my priest, why did you join us? Do you think we still mistrust you?"

The questions took me by surprise: I had not expected this. His welcome and his confession had lulled me.

"You're not sure, hey? Well, that's reasonable. You can't judge an act objectively until you've committed it. First you commit yourself, and later you analyze your commitment. But there are always a few factors that edged you toward the choice. What were yours?"

I searched my memory. My years in the seminary, my term at the Angelicum, my various ministries, my anguishes and disappointments. They did not make a unified whole. There was no consistent thread to mark my path. Reasons and justifications frayed and snapped. For no obvious reason I thought of Shiva, the Destroyer, the Fire. Yes, that must be it. As a youth I had dreamed of immolating myself for an ideal. As a priest I had been ordered to defend institutions doomed by history. Yes, there was the disappointment. I had dreamed of fire. But they had made me a sheep, and sheep do not revolt.

"I hate hell," I breathed, "and this country is a hell now."

"You're a fanatic, my proud Pierre. Being human isn't enough for you, and there's your despair. You're not a sage. Do you know Say? No? All the better for you." He smiled. "Say has solved your problem in a sentence you'll like: 'The fear of hell has produced more stupidities than good works.' Archimedes said he could move the world, only give him a place to stand; the Jesuits solved Archimedes's problem. You're a child of the Jesuits, aren't you? Of course, I know, the Angelicum. In spite of everything the Jesuits are your real masters. Your real problem is that you're a black priest twinned with a colonial intellectual."

He left me. It was cruel. I felt abandoned, dying at the edge of a vast deserted scree. If he held out his hand, I would be saved. . . . My commitment and my act had become ridiculous. The motive for my nationalism lay exposed: I was only a man tormented by xenophobia and racism, who in a sudden impulse had rejected assimilation. So my pretensions were just another charade, and my presence in this camp would only be a stopgap.

And then I felt the immense weight of the wheel about my neck.

In the warmth of my bunk I wished for a miracle. I who had never believed in them now asked for one. An investigation, and a verdict praising my selflessness. An apology would only open the wound, and diminish me unfairly. For goodbye the Colonel had said, "Good luck and chin up." Why? Earlier, showing me the stolen books that were, as he put it, his daily bread, he had slipped these unexpected words into an innocuous explanation: "What Leopold II did was what Cardinal de La Vigerie did." Leopold in the Congo, and La Vigerie in Algeria, the one foolish and the other humane, had both helped impose a strict and brutal colonialism in the name of civilization. "Your move."

Had I fallen into a trap? No: I must not for anything glorify my own defiance—a narcissism that might appease me by disguising the flawed creature that I am. Yet a guilty happiness

pervaded me; I accepted my complicity in the Colonel's ambi-
guities. His name mattered little; he was an impersonality, as I
should be in my priestly role. An object dominated by an idea,
by a state of grace. I'm not sure why I felt so safe and sheltered.
"*Suave mari magno* . . ."

The barracks echoed a multitude of snores. I was on watch.
The uneasiness would lift. I must just go on living my witness.
My moral masochism was also a constant state of actual grace. In
the gloom of the night-lights I tried to find my crucifix, lost in
the leaves. Joy: full swelling joy. A taste of grapefruit laced with
port rose to my throat.

O Lord, I am neither a dancing master, as my people would
have me believe, nor a mischievous child. They talk to me of
negritude and of the emotions that they say define me. Empty
words, Lord, words without meaning in Your kingdom. Help me
to resist this sterile, wasting egotism.

Why must I accept party lines that define You as a mere
tradition before I can become Your servant? I cannot suppress my
ambitions and desires simply because they do not deny Your
message. For the moment, and perhaps forever, I accept the rack
so that these false contradictions may be exploded.

They talk about my slow approach, and they mock me for a
latecomer. You sent me forth into them. True, I come empty-
handed. But tomorrow, Lord, tomorrow I, too, hope to offer You
thanks in the hum of machines free of racial peculiarity.

That is why I want so much to join in preparing a world
under Your rule. These preparations corrupt me, because I must
kill those who use You and falsify Your message. Help me not to
despair. And to open the way for You through my own agonies.

I dream, Lord, of a communion of traditions, a marriage
between poets' hearts and laborers' hands. A communion more
faithfully in Your image. So, dear God, please accept this testimony of my hatred for hell on earth, and of my own madness,
which I accept for Your greater glory.

5

"You were fantastic, Pierre. I mean it."

"Oh, don't exaggerate," I said, rather annoyed.

"All right then, you weren't. If that's what you want. There's your bad conscience at work. But strip away the humility and you'll see what you're really like."

I admit the truth of that. My own truths won't do now; I leave them unformulated. I'm afraid of them. I'm afraid of too much pain if they dominate my mind.

And what are my truths? The end product of all the restrictive myths that bind me to an archaic world? At any rate something is shattered. A fog has thickened, and for some hours now I have been plunged in shame: I led a massacre in the grand manner.

He was alone as usual. A colonel. No: the Colonel. Why does he keep to himself? Asceticism or vice? "My time is the future, Pierre. Your priesthood of blood helps keep me alive. It will get you nowhere yourself, of course. But isn't it more important to live reality and not symbols?"

"No. On the contrary, I want to accept symbols. I risked my
life—I hope that isn't meaningless."

"What would it mean?"

I contemplated the Colonel. My colonel. I was horribly
afraid. Not of my solitude, full of a wild hope after all, but of this
man.

"He is a *shikwembu* (ancestral god)," my old grandmother
told me. The man too was ancient. "For more than five times
fifteen rainy seasons I have drawn water from this river that
preserves us. And that man has always been old, silent, and sad."
Dried wood: I thought of the cursed fig tree. "He is a *shikwembu*,"
my grandmother said again. "No one else on earth is quite like
him." Like my colonel.

My kingdom is not of this world. And yet it was in this
world that His kingdom began, with the Incarnation. Death was
a simple passage: a ritual, as for the *shikwembu*. I contemplate my
colonel.

No, he is not old. His expression is not disagreeable: it
foreshadows some other look. He was the first to speak to me
without perplexity of the fear of hell. Birds break into morning
song; dawn is upon us. I slump in sudden exhaustion. Just as in
Rome. After more than ten years my fatigue recalls mornings
during exam period, when the same invincible weariness bowed
my body and sharpened the irresistible aroma of coffee that
haunted me throughout the service. Coffee: liberation in each
hot mouthful. Father Howard drank it black and without sugar.
At first I made fun of him. Dishwater!

"No, Pierre! Sugar spoils good coffee. Try it. You'll see."

I tried it. A bad taste the first few times. I even suspected
him of trying to save on sugar. But not for long. One morning I
was the first to arrive at our little refectory. Keeping faith, I took
no sugar in my cup; Howard would find me breaking my fast with
an honest brew. In the gentle heat that warmed my mouth I
discovered, for the first time, the sweet delicious purity of real
coffee.

"What are you thinking about now? You haven't answered me."

"I'm thinking about coffee. You have no coffee at all, Colonel? A mouthful? I'm half dead. After a night like that."

He smiled, his eyes gleamed, his face broadened as if he were about to intone some solemn chant. The eyes. Yes, the flame in those eyes troubled me. "No, Pierre, we have no coffee. And even if we had, there's no sugar. I doubt if we have a spoonful: it's expensive. Talk to me about symbols."

"I take it without sugar. I'd love it even cold. I'm bushed."

"I told you—there's no coffee. Talk to me about symbols."

I agreed. I seem made for that: to bow, to rise, to kneel. My life seems little more than a fresco of rituals and obedient responses. Now that coffee has come to mind, so has my father. He died in the afternoon. The ceremony of mourning and lamentation followed traditional ritual. Over the castanets and the shimmering throb of gongs soared the wails of the weeping women. My mother, naked to the waist, a loincloth about her hips, stood close to the corpse. Shrieking, hands stretched high, she invoked heaven and earth. The relatives, squeezed into a corner, also keened, in relays to keep the wailing strong and fresh for the time required by custom, in that sacred obverse of our daily lives. Outside, many men—friends, relatives, strangers—seated on whatever was handy, drowned their obligatory sorrow in the free *malafu,* beer fermented from maize. I was there with them, uncomfortable and nervous in my priest's skin at an animist funeral, troubled and unhappy in the shame and embarrassment of the assimilated man obliged to conform to a ritual he considered only tricks, without true depth and unfortunately without dignity either. My mother exploded from the hut; she had gone mad. She flung herself to earth, matting herself with sand. Within the hut women shrieked as if their throats were about to be cut. In my shocked modesty before these half-naked women I had tried to raise my mother from the earth. Unsuccessfully.

"Leave her there," said my elder brother.

"This is all stupid. I'm as sad as she is. She's carrying on for appearance sake."

"You have to understand them, Pierre."

"And you all might try to understand me. I'm a priest."

He had just smiled. I was on edge. The bawling in the hut, the men boozing outside, fair enough, I could handle that. Shamefully I ignored the ritual ancestral procession, repeated at half-hour intervals, and was only sorry not to be a Saint Columban or a Saint Boniface, neither of whom would have hesitated a moment to instigate a scandal. I was too fond of my father to do that to him. And could I have survived the resulting uproar? But my vanity had ended in shame. For love of God and His commandments I believe I scorned that stout woman, barely covered by a loincloth, her bosom heaving as she bellowed and rolled in the sand. My neighbors sucked modestly at their *malafu* and cast discreet glances at what I considered a horrible farce. Long afterward, in a young people's circle of Catholic Action, when we were discussing customs to be purified in the light of Christianity, I told them about this wake, without saying that it was my father's; and I added, in the ecclesiastical tone of the period, "That farce had less style than a good strip-tease."

Immediately I reeked of shame. Yes: my shirt was soaked through.

I had looked my brother in the face, outside the hut: "Why must she do that?"

"Because we've been cursed terribly: there's no sacred salt in the house. Not a pinch."

I stared at him, amazed. Even he, an educated man, believed in all this nonsense.

The sacred salt, that permits a happy voyage from one life to another, with the mouth blissfully holy. I detect a central region of signs and symbols. Coffee became a rite of passage for me. From the weight of my fatigue to the artificial euphoria of an inoffensive drug. I am denied it now. A curse?

He's still watching me, still balanced impressively between
instinct and reason. A true union of the senses! His reading is as
simple as a cross held before one's eyes.

"Pierre . . ."

He calls to me, draws me up from my fatigue, gentles my
weary delirium.

"Pierre, my little priest, our risks are always heavy. But we
cannot interpret a sign until it is given. Dogmas and eternal
verities reduce anguish to stereotype far too conveniently."

"That may be, but I wouldn't have minded a cup of coffee.
There: I've been frank. Right now, that's what's on my
mind."

"That's a sign too. We might have been able to stockpile
coffee. At times like this it would do us good. But we had to
choose. Not between coffee and ourselves, but between slavery
to a habit and the legitimacy of a drama."

"First we have to be sure where the real drama lies. And
even if absolute selflessness isn't drama . . ."

"None of that, Pierre." His face has closed slightly. He
scratches his left cheek with his right hand, thumb at the corner
of this mouth. His eyes narrow; he inspects me. He continues:
"Never ask yourself useless questions. A priest accepts himself,
Pierre. Forever. Yes, forever. Do you know that? Do you know
that, priest?" He's still smiling, "Priest by order of Melchizedek.
Suscipe me, Domine. Do you remember? Well then. Doubt all the
ways and means of incarnating your dream, but never doubt your
priestly vocation. That would be immodest, wouldn't it?"

The memory returns, insistent. The *shikwembu,* more vivid than
before. I sink into Purgatory with that man. Nothing can foul me
ever again. It is like drink or drugs: they complete the man by
altering him. Why turn down this chance? To be transformed by
a metamorphosis that betrays nothing I hold dear. If an apoca-
lyptitis is what will do it, so much the worse. To live out a series
of consecutive sincerities in real time. But when the immunity
finally failed me, would I still be pure? Purity is essential to a

Christian. Yet when an idea is preserved, isn't its form unim-
portant?

My Spiritual Director at the Angelicum, to whom I confided the morose delectation, the sexual yearning, that became
hallucinating in summer, had led me out of the swamp: "Sex is
not the classic capital sin they say it is, but one among many.
There are some more serious: the sin against the spirit, for example. Your problem is neither exceptional nor extraordinary.
Hold fast to your aspirations, and raise your bodily existence to
their level. There is no true chastity or purity without that urge,
that healthy desire to complete oneself in the feminine. And you
know too that purity can lead to ecstasy. You must beware of that
as much as of orgasm's revelation. In the one and in the other,
there is an expense of life in an offering which, at a certain point,
becomes irrevocable because it is accelerated by a call beyond our
powers. The saints were not composed wholly of spirit."

It was as well: he had rescued me from an *idée fixe*: the
human body scored and scarred by original sin. Too cruel a
metaphor. Much too cruel and for no good reason.

" 'Mastery of the body,' " he told me, " 'is an unfortunate
phrase, the product of a certain era. The Church had to take
some stand on physical love. The phrase was born. There is a
smuggled assumption to be discussed. And modern psychology . . .' "

The road to take, unswervingly: establish the noncontra-
diction between Faith and Modernity. The Church and the spiritual expectations of all mankind. The encyclical letter *Evangelii
Praecones* had not long before overjoyed me, but was it anything
more than a truth (most stylishly expressed) defending itself
against opportunistic couplings—opportunistic but justified in
advance by the message? Form betrays. Form *can* betray. What
matter, if the eternal meaning retains its true value?

Right. Rome. An autumn afternoon. A Wednesday. Visiting Santa Maria della Vittoria in search of silence, I discovered
Saint Theresa of Avila in the Cornaro Chapel. A chapel is a

gentle appeal to the senses: the declarative altar, the subtle physical curve of the columns. The play of sunlight blending with passive metallic lines. And there, dominating the sacrificial altar, Theresa of Avila as offering, crushed in her own flesh. The inexpressible ecstasy has softened her body, which yields, consenting, the eyes closed, the mouth open, one hand and one foot limp, melting. And before this ecstatic suffering, this love beyond which no love can exist, the angel—radiant, smiling, the arrow in its hand, its head lovingly tilted—acknowledges the gift before witnesses: the Cornaro family.

The voluptuous sensuality Bernini so scandalously depicted in this statue was a revelation, helping me to accept my own desires and to love the *pensée* of the great mystic of Avila—which lectures in Asceticism and Mysticism had so badly misinterpreted at the Angelicum. The professor, a Dominican dry as a fishbone, destroyed the mystique masterfully, explaining it by psychology, psychoanalysis, and even parapsychology. From absurdity, the eternal glory of the Church sprang forth renewed: all that is to come has been since time immemorial borne within the experience of the Church.

"My little priest is very tired."

Not even my mental wanderings surprised him. "And you aren't?"

"Less than you, I think. There's a happiness in becoming a truth unto oneself. No further need to think."

The Colonel was tempting me. A phrase leapt to mind: "What is truth?"

He broke into laughter, a vulgar bray that irritates me. For no serious reason: I only find it unseemly. But why shouldn't a colonel be entitled to a fat, happy laugh now and then?

"What is truth? I'm not sure. I may disappoint you. My master, Marx"—he smiled emphatically—"wrote to Ruge over a century ago, and I quote from memory: 'We do not approach mankind as dogmatists to bring them a new principle. We do not

proclaim "Here is the truth: fall to your knees!" From the principles on which the present world is based, we are developing
new principles. We do not say to them, "Stop your squabbles;
they're foolishness; we now offer the correct order of battle."
What we do is to show them why they fight. They will then
decide for themselves whether they wish to cease and desist.
Changing men's minds consists simply of opening those minds,
waking men from their self-centered dreams, explaining their
own actions to them.' That's what we're trying to do here; what
you're trying to do too."

I was indeed disappointed. "But—"

"No, Pierre, I know. You might be happier if I told you that
for you, truth is the tension between your own inner hells and
the world's visible hells. Apropos, are you happy?"

"I think so, yes. I think I am."

"Then why are you ashamed of what you stand for?"

Arguing with him is a nightmare. He consoles me, shocks
me, accepts me as a friend, and then rejects me firmly and coldly.
The little snares he sets strangle all my scholasticism. How can
I answer him? if not by exhaustion. After a sleepless night my
mouth is sludgy. Antoinette is already asleep. A curious pair of
commandos. We accomplished our mission. Admirably, he told
me. And yet I am ashamed. Of the success or the bloodshed?
The sun is rising. But the fierce fever of nature reborn will not
warm me today. I almost regret it. "I'm tired, Colonel."

"Go and sleep. But come back. Let me know by Garbage
Girl. I'd like to go on with these little debates. Well now! You've
been here fifteen minutes and you haven't made your report. Tell
me quickly: I'm listening. Later today you can submit it in writing. So?"

"I had a map of the region with me. Bidoule had lent it to
me. We moved out as planned at one in the morning. When we
reached—"

"Hold on a minute. What do you think of Antoinette?"

"Very effective. Even so, I wonder why you assigned her to
me, especially for that sort of mission."

It had shocked me. The priest and the woman. Roommates. Picture us chatting innocently during the siesta. The mood is already thick: I'm certainly fond of her. But being jammed in with her by order is an atrocious humiliation. Why? Not for anything would I have agreed to compromise any woman in the camp.

I protested to Bidoule, "Pair me with a man. It'll be easier all around." I was pleading.

"Because you'll feel less responsibility, I suppose. You'll march with Antoinette. Anyway I can't do a thing about it. Orders."

This deliberate manipulation of human feelings had surprised me. And disgusted me during the raid. Now, as then, I could only lodge a mild protest.

"They threw Antoinette at you, as you put it, because you need her," the Colonel went on. "You need a Virgin for your salvation and a woman for your manhood."

So that was it. A bleak and deliberate calculation. Stupid. But, in fact, what was so stupid about it? It was normal and reasonable. They had observed me, studied me, stripped away my veils. The pure Virgin of my shy and chaste innocence had been assigned to me as comrade-in-arms. In the form of a living woman, with her sweat and her weariness, her fear and her nervous intuition. This incarnation would bring her down from behind the altar and set her close beside me. And in return for that real presence, to show thanks for the grace of her vulnerability and the variety of her gifts, I would be at once a disciple of Lancelot and of Marx. "You're saying you have no confidence in me, not yet. You've issued me a mirror in which I can read my own treacheries from time to time. And you know how afraid I'd be to betray under those conditions."

He smiled. He made no excuses. It is not the complacency of the infallible. Once more he seems to understand my pain, but blithely erases it, as he would a faint pencil line. "Tell me about the raid, Pierre. You see symbols everywhere."

I tried to go on, strangely out of breath. Fatigue. Physical fatigue and above all moral. "Reached Kilanga at two in the morning. Right on schedule. The sentries were asleep. There were three of them at the gate. We disarmed them."

His eyes were gleaming again. His little grimace. His right hand went to his cheek, the index finger scratching gently and the thumb at the corner of his mouth.

I went on: "I decided it was useless to kill them. We knocked them out, clubbed them."

"Who?"

"Antoinette."

"Go on."

"First we headed for the arsenal. I set the charge. There was nobody around—we'd expected that—but a few steps away we almost had trouble—a soldier, with a woman and drunk. I bashed him, knocked him out. But the woman's screams—Antoinette was gagging her—worried me. We waited two minutes for the arsenal to blow. Nothing. I went back inside. I had to pull the detonator out of the dynamite, repair the wire, and set another charge just behind the big barracks about ten meters away. That blew three minutes later. We were a hundred yards off, with the soldier. I think the whole place was leveled. We only saw one man in the flames, running and waving. We marched almost ten kilometers farther from here, in the other direction. At about three-thirty we interrogated the soldier. He was a captain. He told us so, and threatened us. We made him talk. Nothing of interest. A spineless fool."

"How did you do this?"

"We made him itch."

"Who did?"

"Me."

"How?"

"There were red ants. I sat him down on the anthill."

"And afterward?"

"He died."

"Not of red ants; not so soon."

"I killed him. Those were the orders."

"Did you hear his confession first?"

My gorge rises. I fight it. No use. I turn away and retch. Ashamed, I raise my eyes to him, fearing to find pity in his own. No. Nothing in his eyes. But their metallic, icy quality has clearly, if almost imperceptibly, thawed toward friendship. I am about to thank him. What can I say?

"Sleep till noon, Pierre. It's the usual thing after a raid."

So the garrison at Kilanga no longer exists. By my faith or my lack of faith? Those hundreds of corpses left in the sun do not detain my attention. Distant hecatombs, consuming only strangers, even when they shock me do not carry the impact of one man whom I have spoken to and who dies before my eyes. Something of myself dies with him. Is that a weakness? I feel nothing. Absolutely nothing but my enormous fatigue. The captain? He looked too much like the priest at Kanga; no regrets. At least at the moment. Afterward. It's always afterward.

Antoinette was weeping. Why? It was certainly not the first time she had seen death by violence. My eyes stung badly; I could not linger on this defeat of divinity. "Forget it, Antoinette. Tomorrow death will be the exception again, like a bad dream, in a new nation. And the captain was a braggart; he died of his own stupidity. He'd had too much to drink. It was suicide."

That was not true. I lied deliberately, so that another's death might bring forth peace. To be an exotic bird, caroling away on an isle of treasures. I was in truth drifting between tides. Armed and disarmed, outlaw and just man at once.

It was a quarter of four: I had to make my way back to camp before sunrise. That was an order. I took her by the hand. "Come, sister." The climb was easy in the miracle of my repentance: no victory chant for me. Nor dirge either. "My sister." Yes: I needed this confusing no-man's-land where feelings blurred the truth of actions. In her kindness Antoinette

helped me not to draw back from my own extremes, or deny my
sticky conscience. The Ascension.

I envied other ascensions. John of the Cross and Theresa of
Avila, Vincent de Paul and Louise de Marillac; Francis of Sales
and Chantal. Our own was oddly like a descent. Instead of
nourishing and enlarging life, as their love had done, ours destroyed it, under a sadly logical pretext—the uncertain hope that
life reborn would be better. Panic. The Bible. Surely: *Cum justis,
justificaberis et cum perversis perverteris,* the Psalmist sang. No
exegete would offer me that cold hope. The prophetic tone of
Victor Hugo's *Contemplations* distracted me: "In dreaming, man
descends to the universal abyss." What is an abyss, Lord? To
descend, to lose oneself in it, would be a kind of peace.

I had yet a free hand, and in the gloom I offered it to remedy
the irremediable: Antoinette's vertigo. Her weakness in the
lamplight frightened me. My hand, given in friendship, calmed
her; and I would not share the perpetual doubt that was breaking
my heart.

I began Prime, and held out as far as the first verse of the
hymn:

> *Stars and the night have given way to the day*
> *Let us pray to Almighty God*
> *That in our acts during this day*
> *We shall set our hand only to innocent works.*

That last line buried me alive. How could I hedge myself
about with tricks and not be tricked? From the depths of centuries of ancestral wisdom, I could dig up only one trite sentence;
it would not provide a moment's surcease. *You can build a canoe
with wood, but not with iron.* In the past I had sadly neglected my
ancestors. They would not rally to me now.

All I had to work with was Antoinette's despondency,
which deepened my own.

6

THEY'VE SHOT SOMEONE. I NOTE with interest that I am fortunately not accustomed to it. Or not yet. I react badly to a disciplinary execution—it is an assassination committed in the name of Moloch. But the myths of the people's revolution stand secure. A faithless partisan has been smelted back to ash. His crime? Treason: he left camp at night without permission of the authorities. The usual self-criticism was therefore not sufficient to wash away his sin. Certain lapses here would seem to be inexpiable. I asked if I might be present. The Colonel was all scorn: "Your presence would only sanction weakness. If you want to go on feminizing the men, do it on your own time."

The condemned man also rejected me. "Get out." "I don't need anybody." "Anyway you're a false priest." "Anybody but you." The protests were merely annoying. What vexed me more was his useless death. For all I knew he *did* want a priest, and I was not good enough for him. Too bad. But I wanted—so fervently!—to exercise my ministry. For him, but for myself too.

The ritual would have cleared an obvious space between my comrades and me. They would have seen me in another light. The sacred must keep its distance to survive. And that brave fool frustrates me. He's left me with a bitter aftertaste. Antoinette and Garbage Girl were there. For them most of all I wanted to be the link between the condemned man and God. Why deny it? For them most of all. My role, played out in public, might have soothed the first and brought me closer to the second, whom I wanted to be able to love—as a priest. God denied me that consolation. His will be done.

The lure of another world obsesses me. The silence of a meditation face to face with Him. An impossible confrontation? I could wish to learn life again, closer to Him. I might reveal my truer self then, and my desires might match His demands perfectly. Just to leave this place, to flee, would be enough. The rot in our present world keeps me here. A love of justice too. And my own nature, which somehow I cannot love, is probably my equivalent of the Stations of the Cross.

"If you want to go on feminizing the men . . ." O Lord, I would rather subdue them, as You have. Teach them to love Your delights and demands. Those are within reach of our intelligence. What would become of us if You were not there? Charity, love, would be heartbreaking without You. Working for future generations is well and good, but what answer do we make to our own death? The death of this executed militant? Marxism evades these questions. The joy in my heart, when I think that only You can still comprehend this man whom we have repudiated! Thank You, Lord. And help me follow the path I have chosen to bring me closer to You.

"Feminize the men . . ." Not bad. I remember Sanguinetti: "Pure reason, sure judgment, loving charity nourished by the word—that is how we see the truth and work for the rule of God. It would be wrong for reason to grasp reality only through the senses, only as it exists when perceived." He was picking at Heidegger's flaws, reproaching him for the absence of any spontaneous sense of reality capable of recognizing spiritual distinctions. And from those purest abstractions Sanguinetti fell into everyday banality, pleading the case for Scripture. That sort of dogmatism shielded me in my thought as in my life. And thanks to this cautionary reminder, I have just spurned the Colonel. How valid is it really?

Fabrizio wondered prudently, "My dear Pietro—I cannot understand why we in the Church cultivate a philosophy of hopelessness."

"Hopelessness?" I was astonished.

"We attack, we slash, we insult. To us there are only heretics, psychotics, imps from hell, or evildoing vipers."

That was Sanguinetti's language. The structure of his courses, solid when it came to interpreting Plato or Aristotle, Saint Bonaventure or Saint Thomas, grew flexible and evasive at the edge of non-Catholic thought. And insults sparked; entertaining at first, they soon made us uneasy.

Would he recognize me now? The one time he received me, in his tiny office, I left full of piety, in a state of grace. He was the same as always, generous. Except that his eyes were even gentler in their steady gaze: "Pietro, the spirit of God is abroad in your land. It is a great happiness to the Church."

"Yes, Monsignor."

"Over five hundred parish priests, and two local bishops. What a benison!"

"Yes, Monsignor. It is a great blessing."

"It is indeed. When the first harbingers of Christ came to your country, violence and barbarity still reigned; it was a time of slavery and human sacrifice. I've read the books—Baunard, Lechaptois, Roelens. God keep them, could they have imagined that in less than a century you would be here?"

". . ."

"The Lord works in mysterious ways. Are you happy in Rome?"

"Yes, Monsignor, very happy."

"And we're very happy with you. My colleagues think very highly of you. Your ready intelligence, your sure judgment, your

sincere faith. Continue in that path, Pietro. Be stout of heart:
the Church and Africa are counting on you. Remember the
parable of the talents."

The parable of the talents. Can the Church still count on
me? I would have hoped so then, and I hope so now. But the
important thing is that Christ count on me. And Africa? Which
Africa was Sanguinetti talking about? The Africa of my black
colleagues, doing very nicely for themselves, or the Africa of my
relatives, who already call me traitor? Would he have meant the
Africa we defend in this camp?

I had suffered great love, great desire. And then all things
were permitted, in my new freedom, as long as I did not yield to
temptation and reaffirm the compassionate virtues. Being a priest
must pay. How trite and foolish! Yet only a few months before I
would not have dared think it, much less say it. Being a priest
pays off. And handsomely. In colonial times a priest, even a
black priest, was somebody. Somebody *different*. Intellectually he
moved in circles that allied him with the masters. He was accepted. He knew that by his priesthood he had broken through
a barrier. His life, offered to the divine embrace, was lived in a
constant glow of human happiness. He was no longer classed
with the damned. He enjoyed a signal honor: he could intercede
with God for any man, even a colonist.

The Fathers in the minor seminary made melodramatic and
minatory scenes about it. We must shape ourselves perfectly to
this use. To be expelled from the seminary was a profound disgrace, the most heinous. God's call in our young hearts was also
a call to a dream fulfilled: a social status that we could aspire to
only in the priesthood.

"There are cheats among you who have come to the seminary to study: only to study."

The Father Superior stormed and fulminated. The same
accusation recurred so insistently, so regularly, that it must have
scarred us somehow. At least by teaching us that in our country
the way of God was still the only path to knowledge. A miraculous path. Knowledge arrived with the miracle that was God.

Longing for the divine thirst was twinned to worldly ambition.

The priesthood pays. Why shouldn't I admit it now? My exile frees me to say it and helps me purify myself. Doesn't God work in mysterious ways? My master's in Canon Law and my doctorate in Theology were to open an empire to me. For a priest, worldly glory is still the glory of God. I might have accepted it with the proper trembling and humility: "There are many more worthy than I, but if it is God's will, I accept."

And how long could I have lived with such hypocrisy? Perhaps there exist rare virtues buried among worldly honors. If God Himself were hidden among them! Would I have met Him there, though I seek Him in the shadows where, it seems, He most willingly offers His grace?

"My dear Pietro, what would you like to do after your studies?"

"I will happily do whatever my bishop commands."

"What would you prefer?"

"Oh, you know, Fabrizio, a little country parish."

I was lying. Yes, I lied, and urged humble service. Only apparently humble; after all, a country parish is still a pleasant bourgeois life, a privileged life for the heart and soul. I was lying: I had no desire for that inconsequential existence. A shallow little life! In my own country I dreamed of being a professor at the major seminary, thanks to my degrees. Why not? Many who teach have only their master's.

"But some day you may be a bishop. Many young Africans who study in Rome become bishops."

I rejected Fabrizio's suggestion with horror. Fell back on my parish, defended it heatedly. I knew Fabrizio was right. Did he envy my lot? But I found his suggestion uncommonly intoxicating. O Lord, I thought, Thy will be done. But I clung to my dreams of success. To break through as a bishop was success. If even at the price of a holocaust God should offer me the trappings of empire, why should I reject them, after answering his initial call?

I was a professor at the major seminary. I shall never be a

bishop. Even my professorship will have been only a detour on the road of God's service. The bush has isolated me. I had hoped it would offer me the serenity of Paradise. I have found in it, as I have found everywhere else, glimpses of my soul, of my own heart's generosity. I have love to offer. But how can I be sure the offered love will be accepted? Our landscape here is a living silence: the chirp of birds and insects, the rustle of leaves. That's all. I wonder if I'm more real, in this isolation, as a priest and an African. If I deceived myself at the start, and am lying to myself now, am I justified by the honest intent to survive my present self and become other? Continuity. A royal tour of my virtues!

I love. What do I love? The misgivings that torture me, or the God who shocks and offends me because he reminds me more and more of an insurance company? Perhaps he left us long ago. And my program is an attempt to catch up with him. Like that man just executed. Didn't God reject me there?

I tell myself it doesn't matter. That's not true. Scripture consoles me. All men lie. Where does that get me? "My world is the future," the Colonel told me yesterday. If only I could commit myself to it fully, without remorse or regrets! Confess my anguish, the pain of searching for sense in empty ritual, even as symbols still move me to the core. I am a bit like the missionary-martyrs. They flung themselves into the unknown. Barbarism, as Sanguinetti called it. The crown of martyrdom followed, in the natural order of events. The difference is, I am outside that order. In preaching the word, they also taught worldly values. Missionaries and civilizers. The path of pride. Yet my resemblance to them holds only on the level of aims: I fling myself into an adventure in the name of an abstract love we both profess. But I bring no established truth; I have seemingly no established civilization to impose. On the contrary, even I have still to embrace fully the truth of my new system. But there are no guidelines. My case is too different. Can a theology of violence or revolution—my own goal—even exist within the Church without condemning her? Christ would survive it. But the Church?

7

MISSION WITH GARBAGE GIRL.
I've become a ladies' man.

Empty . . . no more warning signals. When my stomach contracts it only means I'm hungry. Moral turmoil and spiritual panic have subsided, still there but sharply reduced. How do my eyes look to others? When I was young I hoped for immaculate whites of the eyes. Handsome. Now they must be red from lack of sleep. Even if the path chosen is the path of virtue, there is no escape; nor can one escape the whites of one's eyes.

I am beginning again.

The weather is fine. On this new path I feel keen pleasure. My routine and its meaning fall away from me, from my body at rest or bored or exhausted. Love of nature is a dormant taste buried deep within me. Is this new outlook a retrospective view of my whole universe? My origins call to me, in a whisper.

How old was I? Seven or eight? My father's brother had taken me under his wing during vacation. "We must bind him to the real world, before other powers take him," he told my father. And in

truth I was about to start school. Despite my baptism in the
Catholic Church, or perhaps precisely because of it, this initiation was to score my soul.

The high priest, his body painted red and white, a lion's tail
in his hand, danced rapturously to the tintinnabulation of tiny
bells and the muffled beat of the sacred drums. Barely clad,
unsexed by the paint, he prayed to our forefathers, calling upon
my tutelary ancestor Landu, the great-grandfather of my mother's brother.

The prefatory prayers ended, they sacrificed a goat. Now the
silent participants were at one with destiny. Their ancestors had
granted their prayers. The poverty of this initiatory sacrifice
served also to tighten the bond between the living and the dead.
My uncle held the hind hoofs, another relative the forefeet. The
priest jerked the goat's head up by a sharp tug on the horns, and
plunged his knife into the beast's neck. Blood spurted, a red
fountain; I had to soak my hands and feet in it. The dances
resumed, this time on the village common. Joyful, delirious,
shattering the silence. All desires were anticipated, as I was to
learn later; expert feet made fine display in dances exalting blood
and the luminous flesh.

In a hut the priest confirmed me in the ancestral faith,
escorting me into the preconscious. "The world is one as Majewa
[God] is unity. The source and fount of all, he gave birth to his
own creations. To be a man is to become a man. You have all
your life for that. You are only a name in the night. Your ancestral namesake has given you life by his power. Your freedom
will be the freedom to be a loyal man, feeling and reflecting our
past. What you are, is all. An all living by the lives of all. This
all unites complex elements like the beds of our rivers and the
hearts of our enemies. The power of life, brutal, which links you
to the holy rhinoceros; the intuition of life, which interprets the
exuberant powers about you and warns of evil; the rigid will that
finally sets you on your own path under the sun. You will be a
force if . . ."

The words flew through me, mysterious then. I'd have liked them better now. My confirmation then only exiled me from my own people. I was required to drink a small spoon of fresh blood; it discouraged me. I needed tidier symbols. Less obvious, more civilized. Or so I believed.

But the wine at Mass said less to me, like the consecrated wafer I learned to munch lightly, my hands joined and my head bowed. I thought I had taken a great stride forward. But the step was too short, the transition free of mystery because too direct. It was too true to a past still quite close, even as it plunged me into a future that offered fulfillment. The symbols themselves were frankly too austere.

The landscape here is like my thoughts—sinister in its monotony. Stunted sad trees, spared by the sun. On the horizon, bald hillocks commenting comically on the luxuriance of tropical lands. Much sandy soil. A few boulders. A few termites' nests, shapeless. The sky was clear, gleaming blue in almost irritating purity. A renunciation. I thought, "At least the sky brings me closer to God; the heavens proclaim His glory."

Suzanne is a silence. Wrapped in her own thoughts, she ignores me. Her woman's clothes, donned for the occasion, have softened her. But she remains closed to me. My poverty of mind urges me toward her. What is she thinking about? She seems perfectly stable and predictable. I'm jealous. After all, if we have to spend a few days together we may as well say hello—even if I must humble myself.

"Is it still a long way, Suzanne?"

"We'll be there by mid-afternoon. You don't know this territory?"

"Yes, fairly well. But I've lost the knack of walking."

". . ."

"Listen, my dear—may I call you my dear?"

"Why not?"

"The diocese owned cars and motorbikes. I used them."

"I wasn't criticizing."

The shame of not having been poor. At home I was; not destitution, but extreme poverty. In Rome I learned poverty of the spirit. In the theological sense, that implied the pale taste of a sublime and soothing disgrace. All one needed was to sense the conflict between present and eternal life in the Beatitudes. To live wholly in the present, yet sense the extravagance beyond. Sanguinetti even gave a course on poverty of the spirit among princes of the Church, condemned in the sight of all to transformation by garish riches.

"You're too hard, Suzanne. On yourself and everybody. We have to cling to the poetry in our dreams. But you stamp it out. In the end you won't care."

"Oh no. The virtuous middle way. That's just laziness. A good militant ought to know—"

"I know the partisan's catechism as well as you do. But I still wonder. If we want to make a happy world, don't we have to salvage some of our victims' virtue?"

"Then you're not a Marxist?"

"I'm trying to be. I really am. Just as I'm trying to be a good priest. Or more to the point, a good Christian."

The sun was higher. Stifling. I am ambivalent about my Africa. I have tasted the sweetness of a snowscape. Known the seductions of intimate climatic variety. The heat of Rome drove me to the lakes of Lombardy. Transparent sensual light. Varese, Biandonno, Monato, Comabbio. I was captivated. Six years of Europe, and I'd scarcely seen more than Italy. A short stay in London for summer courses in idiomatic English. I'd returned in four weeks and taken up my pilgrimage: Isola Bella, Isola Madre. And to wallow in earthly devotions.

"Pietro caro—"

The invariable greeting. My young Italian friend, a priest like me but an orphan, was my echo and my shadow.

"Why didn't you like England?"

"It was too much like my own country, Fabrizio."

"Non possibile, come?"

"It's too tidy. Too frank and too free. No love of speech or spectacle or even life."

The cool, sweet air, the dazzling beauty; the return had made me tipsy. As it had Pietro Mastri:

> *Dolci il ritorno per la via che mena*
> *alla casa nell'ora della cena*
> *e del ripos! E là, nell'ombra incerta . . .*

> *[Sweet is the return*
> *home at the time of the evening meal*
> *and rest. And there in the uncertain shadow . . .]*

Subtleties could spring to life here: I had not felt them in Westminster Abbey, nor in Saint John's Chapel at the Tower of London. The choir at Saint Paul's Cathedral looked like some barristers I had seen from behind in foggy Regent Street.

And here, the same starkness. The blinding glare of the sun crushed souls and burned away nuances. As the English fog blanketed them.

"Pierre, did you study philosophy?"

I looked warily at her. A mischievous gambit? Should I draw back or open up?

"I'm not teasing, Pierre. You're unusual. I envy you. I wish I could have studied too. Lots of things. Like you."

The poor woman. If she only knew the depths of my ignorance. Aside from scholasticism; and even there. Like many priests, even university graduates, I had read Saint Thomas Aquinas, but only selections. And of other thinkers even less. Ah yes, Marxism. A few volumes of Marx and Engels that I'd read with the same haste as I had Marius Victorinus's treatises, for my thesis.

With wisdom and power, Sanguinetti lavished obvious truths upon us. "We have had no real philosophers since Saint Thomas. Today, for example: Sartre, Merleau-Ponty, Heidegger.

Literature! Only literature!" He paused, offended and pathetic: "*La pozza* (the pool)." And anyone who showed interest in this degenerate stuff was sent to labor over Canon Moeller's magisterial studies of twentieth-century literature and Christianity.

The handbooks betrayed the same spirit. In particular those on morality. I felt a shiver of fear—if they were so contemptuous of their own, what must they say of us blacks? Were Kant, Hegel, Marx, and all those others only fools?

Shakespeare was right: "We are such stuff as dreams are made on."

"I lost interest. We learn so little, Suzanne."

"Philosophy doesn't help you live your life?"

"It's almost useless. And it's worse when it becomes theology. It only complicated my thinking about God."

"Is Europe beautiful? What's it like? Did you see all of it?"

"You ask too many questions. How can I answer them all? In the first place I didn't see all of Europe. It's big. What's it like? Different."

"Meaning? Beautiful houses, tall buildings, bright lights?"

"Hard to say. There are beautiful houses, in the Roman countryside, for example. And tall apartment buildings in Rome itself. But that's not what I mean. We'll put up the same sort of buildings some day, only more modern. But we'll be different from Europe. More like America, maybe. Only I've never been there."

"Well, what *is* the difference?"

"It's as if each plot of land bore the mark of a man's hand, or each stone was the echo of a spirit, a feeling. . . . Great richness."

The sun discouraged me. I envied people who could ask me to explain Europe's soul even as they trampled on it. That soul so obvious in parades, city squares, holy pilgrimages. Europeans had the leisure to contemplate their own time and place, to understand themselves, to love themselves. Or even to drop out, discreetly and intelligently, doing honor to the same spirit. To tear down Roman art after singing its praises, only in order to celebrate the Gothic or Baroque. To identify with Canova's Paulina Borghese, Titian's color, Dürer's or Grünewald's steely austerity, or Michelangelo's luxuriant artistic free-for-all. Periodically they killed off Homer or Shakespeare and then resurrected him with arguments in praise of a history married to the truth of God.

"The prettiest performance I ever saw was in Rome, Suzanne. A young Italian scholar had submitted a thesis on Homer. You know who he was, don't you?"

"Of course I do. I had a year of high school."

Had I insulted her? No; she was cheerful.

"Go on," she begged, her eyes smiling.

"It took him six hundred pages to prove that Homer's heroes wore beards. Overwhelming evidence in support. It was brilliant. Six months later another Italian worked over the same problem. Opposite answer. Homer's heroes had never worn beards. His work was equally brilliant."

"That wasn't very smart. All you have to say is that we can't say whether Homer's heroes wore a beard or not."

"Which is exactly what a third philologist demonstrated, just as brilliantly."

"A stupid story. Which one was right?"

I burst into laughter. The Colonel: I understood him, a little. I had come out of mourning after a divine transfiguration. After the first Pentecost, the apostles spoke the language of their own country. Each listener understood them in his own language. What was the truth? Which one was right?

"They're all right at once, Suzanne."

And I resumed the happy recital of my own laughter. Euphoria.

We arrived at about four-fifteen. A revealing trip. I had finally met Suzanne; understood her; admired her. The mission had merged with that transitory yet infinite shift.

I tried to pray. I meditated upon the Virgin Mary. It was

Suzanne who had unveiled her for me. In this whores' hotel of a
barracks where I must live with Suzanne, I seek to encounter the
Virgin Mother; her purity transforms me, and I am Dante.

Vergina madre, figlia del tuo figlio umile ed alta più che creatura.
We were in touch, free and uncoerced. Daughter of your son,
Virgin. Extreme purity and exemplary chastity. Clemency made
flesh and Fidelity supreme. Mother eternally Virgin and Virgin
eternally Mother. Immaculate white. At once Ark of the Cov-
enant and Heaven's Gate. Refuge, Consolation, Comfort to sinners and the afflicted . . . Among the tangles and heaps of
unknown bodies in happy oblivion, in the passing repose that
men came to seek in this room, I had become prayer itself. My
fervor restored, I settled into it and passed no judgment on the
fire consuming me.

A Kasala. In honor of a living loved one, my people also
recited a litany of praise. It rose warmly in me, contradicting my
arguments the previous night: "You are Pierre. She is called
Suzanne. You are lovers or man and wife. As you wish. For one
night you rent a room in a special sort of house. Don't be nervous, Pierre; all houses of this kind are seedy. No one will even
notice you. Your real identity is the best guarantee of that.
Suzanne knows what must be done. Pierre, you will do just as you
please. Take a holiday. . . ."

The usual horror did not afflict me. At most I was afraid I'd
be recognized.

"They may know me down there. Especially in that small
village. Every time I was promoted or transferred the local paper
ran a photo of me. And if I were to say that my name was Pierre
Landu . . ."

Bidoule had scarcely raised his voice. "They won't know
you. Cut your hair short, right down to the scalp. And leave your
glasses behind for once. It won't kill you. And your name is just
Pierre."

So all I had to do was sign Janus's eschatological register. I
was Monsieur Pierre. Like all blacks. The new uniform deper-

sonalized us. Our colonizers had made us believe that our European given names, by which we were baptized, were the important names. Monsieur Jacques. Monsieur André. Monsieur Louis. We kept our surnames modestly hidden, like some shameful disease. The "devil's name," as the missionaries called it. We had to swap it for the Christian name, the name of the civilized being we became thanks to the holy sacrament of baptism. Abruptly I remembered my recent prayer. Did I really pray? Were those easy praises of the Virgin any more than my translation of a rare moment of true calm? Or of complacency? I never even thought to ask her help with the traditional "pray for us." And why suddenly the Virgin?

Garbage Girl has just come in. "Can I borrow the bed for a while? I want to lie down. I have to work tonight; I won't be back till late."

I shift to the only chair in the room. She stretches out.

"If I'm not being nosy, what are you going to do, exactly?"

"I'm going out dancing with an officer. You can take me to meet him and then come back and sleep in peace. I'll try to spend the night with him. We're off again tomorrow. But we'll be back soon to blow up this whole garrison."

She was hate personified, secreting gall and death. Once when we had made a halt, I asked her to tell me how her conviction was born. Her words came cold and dry. A dead man. A dream shattered. Money.

"I was on vacation. At Christmas time, two years ago. My father fell sick. I took him into town, to the hospital the nuns ran. He had to be admitted. But I had to pay two thousand francs in advance. I didn't have that much. That was in Charlesville. I live in Kato. It's about twenty kilometers. I sold myself over and over for a whole afternoon. When I went back next morning my father was dead—on the hospital steps. I bought him a coffin with the money. A little later, two weeks I think, Bidoule carried me off. I'm happy now."

I gazed at her. She was asleep. Even in sleep her features

were set hard. Shut. The angel with the sword. A fallen woman?
What is that, fallen? Her confession was the tale of a whole era
raped. She stated it with no remorse. A considerable change
from the masochism, whimperings, and panics of the confessional. That Nordic colleague who had chosen me in Rome . . .
I became the confidant of a string of vices: his confessor. Always
the same: "Bless me, Father, for I have sinned." And he set
about poking at his wounds. Patiently. "I have masturbated."

Breathless, he paused. I followed on, a saintly automaton:
"Yes."

"Many times this week. In the bathtub. The warm water.
Soap on my body. For the sake of my health. I helped it along a
bit and by my weakness broke my vow. Another time the idea
came to me on the toilet. I have a sour stomach. The effort to
move my bowels excited me. I soaped myself. . . . I suffer for it,
I am heartily sorry. Forgive me, Father. . . ."

And the *Absolvo* came automatically. I respected the forms,
knowing that in weeks to come the same tears would be repeated, the same sincere repentance concluding the avowal of
habits probably set for life. I worried. Not so much over the
confession, which is sheer joy for some people, but over the
obligatory remorse. Wasn't he negating confession by negating
sin itself under the weight of his compulsive flesh? I left Rome
just before Easter, to flee those holy vices that they asked God to
underwrite by a sacrament. The two hours of the confession that
I heard each week of the academic year were turning me brutish.
I left the confessional with apples, needles, wooden horses,
leather horses, dice, keys, bulbs, cakes of soap, lumps of dough,
even rainfall juggling before my eyes with mouths, anuses, sexual
organs, and immolated street kids. In the end, confession would
probably be the death of God. Its historic justification had never
seemed convincing. Small matter. But I suffered for my chaste
colleagues, no weaker than I, who fell regularly into the tabooed
sin: the sin of trembling priestly ears pricking eagerly at frisky
turpitudes.

I was in a convent full of nuns, replacing a sick friend. How old was she? The grille showed me only little winking diamonds of face.

"Father, I have yielded to the flesh."

"No!"

She stopped dead. I had broken the rules. I realized that, and quickly recovered from my own surprise. "How many times?"

The awkwardness was dispelled. But her faith was a response to my triumphant curiosity. I listened, dumbstruck and happy, with no regret and no compunction. I was ministering.

Garbage Girl's flinty peace revives my treasons. And my presence here seems another offense to the pure and pious whom I once, in the good old days, betrayed only slightly. Only let them not ask me again to drag God into the pride of organized and sanctioned sin! If they would only repudiate at least this one tarnished sacrament!

The icy-white self-criticism here is good enough for me. Here we draw conclusions from facts instead of settling for a bland compunction, however sincere.

But what do we decide? Suzanne will open herself tonight to a man she despises. For the greater glory of whom? "It does not become the saint," Sanguinetti used to say, "to wallow in the mire. Only pigs prefer it to clear water." I accepted my fate: I was a pig. That was my role. But she? And with her, all the others?

8

I'VE SEEN HIM AGAIN. I NEEDED him, was thirsty for him. Ten at night, bedtime. I asked Garbage Girl if he'd see me. She led me to him. Others' deaths were beginning to weigh heavily. What could I do about it? He was there. "I don't seem to be able to sleep just now," he greeted me.

"Nor I. I need to know peace again."

He looked me over. A riddle. My whole past returned as if embalmed, fragrant, embellished, clean and fresh beneath bunches of lilac, glistening in delight like dew on wild violets, the serene landscape of Botticelli's *Annunciation* in the Uffizi. A villa, peaceful colors, adorned by columns.

The kneeling Virgin, her head bowed. Gabriel descending in his glory, the source of light behind him, its golden rays in harmony with the lines of the ceiling stones. That is what I wish for: I am afraid of these times, when the savagery of cunning triumphs so fiercely.

"You fear the day as I fear the night."

I yielded again. "I shall fight and pray." ("Show me Thy

way, O Lord. Thy will be done. Let me know Thy will, fill my heart with Your justice.") I waited for help from him: let him accept this approach to the blood knot. So he, too, knew fear. I was happy now, and all things were possible: I could accept myself as well, and die in human fear even as I suffered the martyrdom of the Cross.

"Fear is a temptation, Pierre, like doubt. Worse: a curse."

Like the curse that oppresses our people, yet happily drives them toward their future.

I understand the curse—except that I see it as God's male-diction.

I was waiting in a parlor at the bishop's palace, slumped in an armchair. Monsignor arrived.

The game lasted a good while. His purpose was to trap me in my own reservations and force me to acknowledge them. This was divine grace: a call to be faithful to the priesthood and also to civilization. "A truly profound Christianity," he stated con-fidently, "is in permanent contact with the values of Christian civilization."

And there was the source of my affliction. Vastly dismayed, I told myself: The grace of my calling is in permanent contact with a divine curse. His axiom produced black priests and bish-ops, just as it justified bashing the Nigger every now and then somewhere in the world. Or the Yellow Peril. Pretty much the same. I recognized the guerrillas' brutality in a now familiar train of logic: "You cannot be a good African and a good Christian at the same time." That was flat. But wasn't Marxism a challenge to this awkward statement of the obvious?

What I must face up to is the kernel of truth buried within this polemical affirmation. My parents too had long condemned my goals and my life: distractions, to them.

The first time I went back to my village in my cassock, I was greeted by my mother's tears: "My son, you have betrayed us." My father settled for an angry growl. I felt contempt for them. In time, I thought, they'll change. They have every right to hate the colonists. But if they think I've gone over to the other side, they're wrong.

"Mother—it's not what you think. I want to be a priest. I'm not betraying anyone. . . . No, I haven't gone over to the enemy. It's not that at all. . . . You don't understand, Mama. You don't understand at all. I want to serve God. Yes, God—and God has no color. You should be happy to have a priest for a son. Why do you say the white man's God? There is no white man's God. There is only one God. He's the same for all. Mama, listen to me. Mama . . ."

She was not listening. Her tears only stiffened my resistance. I wanted to save her. Saint Monica prayed for the salvation of her son Augustin. I shall be Saint Monica. Let my filial love be a prayer for my mother. I'll be a priest for her, and for all my people. Let them grow into Christianity as the spirit wills. . . . It would be ten years and more before I understood my mother and shared the sufferings that ravaged her.

I stared at him. He waited patiently. "What should I do, Colonel?"

Now he smiled. His right hand went to his left cheek. "So you're torn in two. Is there any sensual pleasure in it?"

"No. I'm in real pain."

"And here I took you for a saint!"

"No. I could never be a saint. I don't even want to be."

A slight tremor of disgust shook me. For me sainthood would be a descent into madness. I was not denying Him, but suffering because I could not see Him except through the stained glass of European cathedrals. Verses of the psalms rose insistently to my mind. Judge me, O Lord; for I have walked in mine integrity. Examine me, O Lord, and prove me; try my reins and my heart. Have mercy on me, for in Thee have I placed my trust.

I was calm as he rose. Calm for the space of a question or two. Then the uneasiness gripped me again.

"Christianity is skillful, Pierre. It is the depositary of a truth not more true than any other, but its strength is that it levels all men to its own condition. They submit. It is powerful, disciplined, and dictatorial, and it knows wonderfully well how to exercise both rifle and benediction; as it also knows how to modify a policy just in time. Look at Teilhard de Chardin, and the cult of tolerance so fashionable these days."

"I can't agree with you."

"Obviously you can't agree, or you wouldn't still be one of them. By the way, are you sure that you *are* still one of them? If you are, why do you come to me for help?"

It was because of my grandmother. The sap of history oozed from the earth as it did from her whole being. The hushed sounds of a village at evening carried serenely across the fields of the kingdom to which she held the keys.

"Men began to forget the Creator's truths. They nourished themselves on peppered banana paste, made manioc stews with meat set aside for their ancestors, and drank *malafu* all day long. So then the Father of men and animals, the Master of the fields and gardens, the Keeper of days and nights, sent down a dreadful rain that lasted months, years, and these years passed one after another. And after that a rooster from another world came and crowed, and one pair of ancestors returned to earth with the eternal truth and life began again."

"The Church," I said, "only wants to ease the way for divine truth: truth congeals quickly, and each generation must explore it again, to understand it. Christ did not reveal it once for all time."

"How true. A truth condemned to be forever provisionally definitive. Every twist and turn of history alters it a bit."

"No: it imposes a new interpretation on the message. As with Marx . . ."

"Yes, I see. But I hope you don't take Marxism for a religion."

"Would I be here if I did? Since I haven't denied my own."

"Your . . . ah . . . your religion. You're a good man, you are."

And we begin all over again. This time he did it deliberately. Obviously if Marxism is a scientific methodology I can't logically fling an emotional stone back at him. I recalled the Marxist theories of spiritual life, relegating all values to the realm of pure interest and need, and denying all transcendence. I discarded them. What difference would it make, an argument like that? I had a tower to rebuild and I needed building blocks. Wherever I found them!

It was in Rome, during the supremely fresh and beautiful days of my new priesthood. Incapable of real thought, I was all tender heart. Fabrizio was with me, between classes. We were waiting for Sanguinetti, who was late.

The unaccustomed delay gave us a chance to stroll the corridors, admiring ourselves in our handsome soutanes. "*Pietro caro,* isn't it painful to be Christian and African both?"

"No, my friend. My parents never understood me, but I don't feel like a split personality."

"How can that be?"

I wondered at his persistence. Why should he insist that I be a man divided? The Church had turned out quantities of priests like me. All colors of the rainbow: Chinese, Indians, blacks, mulattoes. You ran across them in all the congregations gathered in Rome, among their elders in the Faith, the Europeans, Dominicans, Jesuits, Benedictines, canons, Holy Ghost Fathers, oblates, Carmelites shod and barefoot, Franciscans of all stripes, sons of all the saints and the blessed of all nationalities. Irony even produced black White Fathers. And among the nuns it was much the same. My joy in an indivisible soul was not egotistical frivolity, but the expression of an equilibrium in Christ. Our agreement was quite firm. Could not be otherwise. And I was shocked that the renunciation I affirmed, in my intoxicated *caritas,* might be only an intellectual flirtation for some of my colleagues. Christianity was my religion. Mine. And my only religion.

"Surely you tried to blaze an African trail through theology," the Colonel went on, "just as others took negritude as their premise and tried to blaze an African trail to socialism."

His mockery was gentler; I was spared the humiliation I dreaded. It was a fretful evening. He said he was afraid to sleep. Daylight oppressed me; I was ashamed to flee from it once again. Our conversation tonight might, I told myself, be more than simple self-indulgence.

"Some of my fellow priests believe an African theology is possible. Just possible."

I smiled. He understood. Full of charm. My God, to establish just one obvious fact, one defensible dogma! He listened with real interest. "They believe in the possibility," I went on. "With them, thought precedes action. It's as if Plato, before beginning his works, had announced that he was about to invent Greek philosophy; and Descartes, French philosophy. Comical, isn't it?"

"So?"

"So—it betrays a failure."

"Yes?"

"I stand for traditional principles—which, by the way, are confirmed by modern experience. Example: Debray after Castro and Guevara. First practice, then preach."

"Meaning?"

"I don't trust theoretical positions established as first causes or prime movers. Sometimes they're only concessions to fashion, or to myth. Like the African road to socialism. A nonexistent distinction raised to the level of an obscene cult."

"And negritude? African values?"

"Ah yes. Practice. They're only the demands of a masochistic cult that believes blacks are different."

"Masochistic?"

"Yes. Black independence was a matter of simple well-timed support. That support is dissipated; the chances are past. African political leaders may now rejoice in the defeat of their schoolboy dreams. Well done, wasn't it?"

"Ah no, Pierre. You have no faith. That's serious."

Maybe it was. So what if my devotion was only a drop in a well of sentimental love? What matter? Would it ever matter? If my dedication were sharper and shrewder I could dismiss all-purpose formulas, and my individual reactions would be less confused. He knew that, so he was lancing me like a boil. My weakness was a perfect target for his meticulous cruelty. As my arguments grew dizzy and weak, he even invited me to have Faith. He was killing me with kindness. He used principles: contingency, spontaneity, thoughtful reasoning. I was a dying man. Like the Duc de Gourmont, whose confessor was terrifying him with the multiplicity of Christian truths, he turned to his wife: "Is that true, Madame?" "Yes." "Then let us hasten to believe it." Exactly.

Faith. Yes, I considered myself Jesus Christ's priest; but when I had to make peace with my race, I found that I was the priest of another world. And my own people were challenging that world in the name of a negritude that discouraged me utterly with its pretensions to eternal existence. Must I place my Faith in that mystification as well? This multiplication of acts of Faith was frightening.

"Colonel: suppose the Europeans began to talk about 'blanchitude.' "

"They'd make millions happy overnight. Look at the Nazis. And you know Denis de Rougemont's thesis. . . ."

"But from the Marxist point of view? The Second International Congress handed down perfectly clear decisions about national and colonial questions."

"But you yourself talk about Castro. Do you know the Cuban road to communism?"

"Gee! What's the final authority in this camp?" He was plucking me apart. My anger was a form of cowardice, a desperate stand against sophisticated complexity. Always nuances, connections, compromises, polite excuses. Finally a talent for lying. I met his gaze briefly; nervously I stared at his left ear, waiting for my defeat.

"As you must know . . ." He paused. I felt his burning gaze, and glanced up to see a voracious beast. I worried: Just what was he defending? He went on. "As you must know, the final authorities are Marx, Lenin, and Mao—Mao above all. Socialism subsidized does not imply servitude. It is not like the Church. Care to comment on that, my little priest?"

The defense of truth. That was his challenge. And I agreed with him. I was beginning to feel quite tired and looked at my watch: eleven. Antoinette is already asleep. So much the better. I'll do less deep thinking. How can I escape him? I'd been hoping to amuse myself this evening, to forget, but the nervous tension was back; he attacked every certainty I tried to lay before him.

"Pierre, you've argued theses on the colonial question. I order you now to remember forever one clause from one of them: the one that insists on 'the need to combat the reactionary and medieval influence of the clergy, Christian missions, and other elements.' Your job, my son, is to instruct the militants on precisely that point. I can count on you, can't I?"

9

To Monsignor Jaak von Kroes
Bishop of Makiadi

Father:

Father Howard will already have written to tell you
that I am joining the guerrillas. I am aware that I have
acted precipitously and I accept in advance the disciplinary sanctions prescribed in my case by Canon Law. This
letter, which I have written in secrecy, and which I will
try to convey to you by a villager, is testimony to my
submission.

The struggle for intellectual maturity that I under-
went after leaving Rome made me see the need for compromises and adjustments before a display of love can
become an authentic commitment through a deliberate
overt act. And it seems to me that we priests, theoreti-
cians of the soul, should respond to that need in the
conduct of our lives and not merely in our words. So I
understand Saint John when he writes *Qui facit veritatem,
venit ad lucem* (3:21).

Father, I do not write thus as a judgment on my colleagues' conduct, or to justify my own revolt. My letter is only the explanation of a painful progress, of a split in myself slowly brought under control, of a personal belief attacked from all sides so that there remained only one honorable expression of it: direct action.

In my life as a priest I have—first unconsciously and then consciously—lived through successive states of sincere belief. My great regret today is my long adherence to a Christianity which only caricatured the evangelical message, a grand human whole. My people still respect Christianity, and perhaps love it; but that, I believe, is only because it is their sole distraction from bleak daily lives; from that perpetual Hell by which we profit; from us priests, members of a privileged class. Do they really believe in God? In all sincerity, I doubt that—because religion is so often, for them, simply an exorcism of poverty; because they have no choice but to be Christians; and because for the moment they are unaware of other ideals. I cheated for a long time, pretending not to notice that I was really one of them, and that my life was only an imposture.

To the child of my people that I was, to the colonial subject that I was, the wealth of our church was a cushy, downy nest; and my priesthood was a social rank protected by those colonial institutions which I claimed to defend for the greater glory of God.

So I was of one class; and my people were of another. The ties that bound me to the souls in my charge made an abstraction of me. I despised the squalid life of my own people, without truly settling in the masters' camp.

The truth is that my seminary education exiled me bit by bit from my own people. The Occident was the norm, Europe the universal reference. The theological tradition of the Latin Church, Thomism, the orthodox

Roman Catholicism of the Council of Trent, all protected by capitalistic sociopolitical institutions, prepared
me well to despise my people and their beliefs. The brav-
est of the black priests fled to utterly ineffectual but
much favored cults like negritude. My university education, a systematic defense of scholasticism and rational-
ity, foreshadowed my future separation from the
traditions I was already demystifying. My thesis in theology, on Platonic echoes in Marius Victorinus's thought,
was significant. It was devoted to my adoration of the
European world which had plucked me from my dark
pagan night.

Forgive me, Father, if I am blunt. The culprit is to
some extent myself. Faithfully and in no critical spirit, I
embraced the principles of my new caste—principles also
of the colonial powers and a financial oligarchy. The
stigmata of my priesthood promised me eternal ecstasy,
first in this world and then in the next. The slight hu-
miliations I occasionally suffered at the hands of my European colleagues, like submitting all my correspondence
to my superior, or rigorously attending the collective rec-
itation of the minor canonical hours until I took my solemn vows—those brief mortifications meant little to me
by contrast to the ease and opportunities of the life.

I went so far as to criticize, from the pulpit, my
compatriots' first demonstrations for independence. My
European colleagues discovered in me "a valuable inter-
locutor," a man of maturity, a devoted priest with a
strong feel for the Church. My appointment as Spiritual
Father to the seminary was a reward for faithful service,
and a mark of confidence.

You wrote then that you were confiding to me the
future of the clergy in your diocese; that my task was to
create priests with the heart of Christ and the spirit of
the Church. I left the crowded places to breathe the fire

of constancy and the love of ancient rites into the young clerics in my charge. For two years I was an assiduous gardener, cultivating the mystery of vocations and the noble dreams that masked the resinous fermentations of the divine call. A year ago you sent me to renew my bonds with God's people, to prepare myself to be the soul of those crowded places, as you put it to me. I do not know what high responsibility you had reserved for me, after this curacy. But at Koloso, God was waiting for me. The abject poverty of my own people unsealed my eyes, and now my only dream is this: to welcome the birth of a purer social order, in which God's face will not be that of a banker—or even a face sculpted by civilization.

Father, I have found here the peace of desert places. But I am happy, truly happy. Our colonel seems to be a just man, an idealist free (in my opinion) of party affiliations. The atmosphere in camp is one of tolerance— except for the flatly antireligious courses in political theory. I do not believe that all the militants are party members. A good many were recruited by force. Furthermore—and sad to state—few of the troops are volunteers; the party falls back on force regularly to swell the ranks. Yet one thing seems certain: the National Liberation Movement directing this revolution is by no means independent, whatever they claim. The general tone of the camp and the presence of Chinese arms would indicate that the NLM is an obedient communist front, inspired by Peking.

The Church will have to react. Especially here in our diocese, where the Movement seems to have eyes and ears everywhere. A few shock troops from Catholic Action, absolutely above suspicion, might go over to the revolution. If they are sufficiently vigorous to work their way up to the central committee, they alone may be able to save tomorrow's Church in this country.

Father, I had to write and confide in you. This letter brings you my hopes and fears. And believe me, Father, still your submissive son and a faithful priest of
Jesus Christ.

Pierre Landu

P.S. Monsignor, you may trust the man who brings you
this letter. He is one of my friends among the partisans;
he lives far from us, in a village about fifty kilometers
from our camp. He is a simple man and upright, who
retains the faith of a charcoal-maker though he adheres
to the NLM. You may send me a letter by his hand.
Please take care of him. Whatever honoraria are due me
for this last month might help him and his family.

P.L.

10

A FIRE IS SO BEAUTIFUL. IT melts the heart, and marks a pause. It is one of the rare luxuries we are permitted: once a week, on Saturday night, a campfire. That too is a ritual, the only ritual that situates us in time, closes one cycle, and opens another. At each campfire I progress. I try to harden myself a bit more. Not in hatred; hate already thrives within me. But in ideals. Leaning toward the flames, I try to understand all the languages floating up on the fragile warm waft.

The comrades wander about happily, greet one another, make and unmake friendships, trying to express their inner strength. Is the fire sufficient answer to their needs and desires? It would seem so. For them it is an enchanted pause, a childhood world reclaiming them mysteriously, between two bloody weeks.

I understand why the Colonel is never there. He is not one to be refreshed by minor diversions.

I still feel a revulsion at this stark existence, to which I too am condemned. I am like a chaplain watching over nice little Boy Scouts. His job is to preserve their innocence. Mine is to guarantee, mainly by my own behavior, that violence takes a firm grip. How can I set myself apart? I know that I cannot. But I know also that there will be no more laughter for me.

At Venice, in a museum the name of which I have forgotten, a guide speaking of Venice's days of power and glory struck me with one sentence: "When Vasco de Gama showed Europeans the road to Africa and Asia, he was an accessory before the fact to the assassination of Venice." The disturbing words return to me through the storm of flames. They stir a lazy sensual memory: I can summon up the colors of Titian's *Venus of Urbino*. His Flora gives way to Sodoma's tortured Saint Sebastian.

At the moment I am trying to converse with my own flesh. Why ignore it? Let me understand its tensions, its sparkle. Let me recognize myself in it. And by heeding the serpent in my own heart, let me flood out the temple and make it uninhabitable by mankind. That is the gospel. The impossible path. He said, I am the way and the truth and the life. It is all one. Christians, all too human, learned to live out a hellish religion. One encounters it innocent, neatly clad, pure of heart, serene; and up a gentle slope, with no real effort, one rises to Heaven.

They speak of Eternity as if it were a reward, or a stage like those a young girl might pass through in life. They forget Hell. Hell is important. There is no evading Hell, either on earth or in the great beyond. We must accept it for ourselves on earth, but work to make others happy. To accept one's own Hell is to incarnate love. Marx and Engels understood that. But the Church is embarrassed to talk about it. They smile. And they forget that Hell exists, that Hell surrounds us. They prefer to smile at Theresa of Avila's wild, passionate imagination. It is obviously not my place to expatiate on the falsification of the Gospel. Still less to pass judgment on it. God forbid. But one thing seems certain to me—that colonial Christianity, like existentialist or personalist Christianity, is directly descended from the European Middle Ages. I heard far too much about Duns Scotus Erigenus, Roger Bacon, Meister Eckhart, and not enough

about Saint Benedict and Francis of Assisi. That stunted my
early tendency toward a human curacy. "If philosophy, even by
correct reasoning, arrives at conclusions that contradict theology, then it is not theology which is wrong, but philosophy."
Signed: Thomas Aquinas. "I think because I believe. If I did not
believe I should not think." Signed: Bonaventure of Fidenza.
Revelation and authority. Not strictly reasonable. And the conduct of generations to come is ordained by them, for good and
all. My freedom as a child of God is the freedom to be utterly
submissive and faithful, destroying myself to conform to dicta
uttered centuries ago. I do not rebel, knowing full well that in
theology terms mean whatever we want them to mean. That is
the genius of religion. Shocked? Not even that. Only a bit disappointed by the various sects' and factions' claims. They made
mutual mayhem at the time, excommunicating one another left
and right. And then by blandishments, base obsequiousness, and
wily sinuosity, they confirmed one or another doctrine as valid.
Now all has been said and done. In a brave new world it remains
only to live by these doctrines. Easy. Precisely: too easy.

My comrades are singing. I don't even try. I know beforehand that I cannot melt into their sun. I go on fluttering about
the source of light. A butterfly. Amid the harmonies of cheerful
human voices, I knead a dried bird dropping, my eyes shut. It is
indecent to approach Christ in any other way.

"You're far off, Pierre. What are you dreaming about?"

It's Antoinette. She annoys me. Shall I tell her? Why can't
she leave me alone? I need to meditate, to understand the love
in me. But I give in. "I was thinking."

"What are you always thinking about? Doesn't it wear you
out? I always thought people who went to school too long turned
out to be a little crazy."

"Why should you think that?"

"I don't know. Take me: I never think. And when I do
think, it's about nothing at all. I live and that's it. But you—!"

"What about me?"

"You're always by yourself, alone and sad. Like the Colonel."

"Did he go to school for a long time?" I perk up. A morbid curiosity, in fact: I'd like to strip his soul bare, know him completely, pierce the mystery of him. The Colonel intrigues me.

"That's what they say. In Czechoslovakia."

"What did he study?"

"I don't know. Why are you so unhappy?"

"Me, unhappy?" I tried to laugh. It was not a success; my laugh was false as hell. I cut it short and met Antoinette's gaze. She waited, perfectly calm. It's true: too much study warps the mind. Would I suffer so many inner stings and pricks if my own world had claimed me from the day of my birth? Slave to a tradition, I had been emancipated by my baptism, and thenceforth shared the concerns of the just. "It's like this, Antoinette: when you love somebody, don't you think of him all the time?"

"No! That's exhausting. You love or you don't love. Why think your life away? My father used to tell me . . ."

Yes. Mine too. "My son, take care to preserve life. Strengthen yourself and your own people. You will be a man." All one had to do was return to the past, shelter there, seek out the inhibiting wisdom of others, and try to identify with it. Or more exactly, to personify it. And then old age would come, full of the pleasures of rank and promises of godhood. I am becoming sensitive to this woman's slightest gesture. I am fascinated by her eyes. Her left foot twitches.

"Thank you, Antoinette."

She stares, startled. Am I crazy? Not at all. I am thanking her for being there at that moment. Just as I will thank God a while later before laying me down to sleep.

If my acts of grace are a desperate attempt to communicate with God's silence, how much must I owe to Antoinette, a presence more than present in my very flesh! "Antoinette: I don't know if I'm unhappy. You see, my education took me to the other end of the universe; my love of humanity brought me here. So I'm trying to be real. To betray nothing. That's why I'm always thinking."

Her eyes were wide. A question or a reward? I glance at my watch: almost time. The spell will be broken. Why go on? These moments with her are only parentheses. I listen to myself prattle. Obviously differences vanish and my tenderness rises, coloring all. It seems facile.

"Doesn't being a priest change you much?"

"I don't think so. It shouldn't change me. But a priest is first of all a Christian, and being a Christian changes you. Yes indeed. Horribly."

Far too much. Otherwise why have I been such a bad guerrilla so far? I remember the Epistle to Diognetus that Father Howard had me read. The first Christians were ordinary people: "They dress like other men and women. They do not live in villages apart, and do not speak some outlandish dialect; there is nothing unusual in their way of life. . . . They are creatures of flesh but do not live by the flesh. They pass their days on earth, but they are citizens of Heaven. . . . In a word, what the soul is in a body, this the Christians are in the world. The soul is enclosed in the body, and yet itself holdeth the body together: so Christians are kept in the world as in a prison-house, and yet they themselves hold the world together." A presence all-inclusive yet discrete, loving yet silent. What a show we put on these days with our flashy pageant!

I won't alter anything myself. What could I accomplish? But I believe it is Karl Marx who has best personified concerned evangelical love over the last century. The world had to be remade. No one else dared say it. Orthodoxy is so restful. The Church wrapped virtue in such a cocoon that any mental reservation immediately became tentative sacrilege. Comical but not stupid, the notions of that French priest who looked to the Church for coups d'état. Such raw human action might help us Christians to understand how much Christ is God and his Church a pale, flawed reflection.

Am I going gracefully mad?

Antoinette has left, dragged off by real life. She told me about her childhood. It was sad and heavenly at the same time. She had barely any education. "Fractions were impossible. I never got past fractions."

I was thinking about concentrations of power, intellect, education, even virtue. All linked. The accuracy of Marx's analyses was dazzling. A blinding glare.

"There were ten of us in the house. I'm the oldest. I was the only little mama for the young ones. And my father believed that too much study spoiled a woman. Is that true?"

"I don't know. Maybe sometimes."

Inequalities. It was all quite clear. You begin with a liberal economy and its basis, the legal appropriation of productive capital; and the inequalities expand until they comprise everything. The automatic functions of money. Scandals of exploitation. And somewhere a little girl quits school in the middle of fractions. Obviously she's not brainy. . . . It was all quite clear. The world needs poverty, trouble, suffering. Otherwise how can loving charity survive?

Marxism via Christian methodology. All so bleak.

But with the emphasis of exhortation, it becomes fiery. No; many prefer to say that Marxism is a religion. It's easier that way: heresy stands out so clearly then.

Fabrizio had made me climb a terraced hillside in Cortona. Far off on the plain, a mirror: Lake Trasimenus. The sun is setting, oh God! Truly.

"Beautiful, isn't it?"

"It is." And so what? What is beauty? Sunsets and sunrises *should* be beautiful. We admire them for that. So I pretend. And yet I prefer a more subdued and warmer light. Then I can feel my own heartbeat. Dusk, foggy: Fabrizio is trying to bring history to life: Hannibal, the Libyans, the Iberians. Flaminius, consul in 217. Before Christ. In Italy I go back that far, even farther. In my own country I can only go back to the beginning of this century. And whose fault is that? No one's. I should like to have studied history at the university. My bishop needed theologians. The fog. There were about 40,000 Carthaginians, and only 20,000 men under Flaminius. Fabrizio and I are living before Christ. Wonderful. History ruled then; it was not theology appropriating all history's aspirations and distorting its meanings. How satisfying to triumph over time by reliving the luck and depravities of dead men! I teased Fabrizio: "We're studying theology here."

"How? Are you making fun of me?"

"Not at all. Livy read historical chronicles. He interprets them by his own passionate views and freezes them for all time, forgetting the hopes and fears of sixty-four thousand men at the battle of Lake Trasimenus. He wanted theoretical support for a conclusion he accepted beforehand. Isn't that theology?"

"My dear Pietro, if you go on like that you'll end a heretic."

We laughed. That summer many nights echoed our laughter. We were happy, sure that the sun would rise tomorrow. Our own task was only to offer ourselves to the light, the beauty. Italy lends itself beautifully to that sort of communion. It was like a splendid game. "Being a priest is easy for you, isn't it, Fabrizio?"

"And why, my dear Pietro?"

I laughed inwardly. The old cheery joke: "Because in Italy a priest inherits it from his father."

He smiled. Sadly. I understood that I had wounded him by the foolish slur. I hadn't meant a word of it—only wanted him to see that for an Italian, becoming a priest seems so normal that he has a slim chance of any martyrdom but a mystic's. And that kind of paradox is peculiar to religion.

Religion? The original myths had swollen and suffocated the underlying truths. Internalizing them on the one hand and intellectualizing them on the other had created the crushing combined weight. God became man. The dialogue began. A monotheism centered on man led man to read God in his own heart. Clearly all one had to do was extend that sacrilege and Marxism would become a religion, like racism or Nazism.

We were in Rome. I was completing my thesis. I attended

every meeting and debate that touched on Marxism at all. Fabrizio came with me, wholly enchanted by the Marx he was discovering. We were trying to understand this version of love for humanity. Each meeting was a step forward, and each return a mortification. Heaven seemed less and less the true call. I knew what was in store for me: the true call was worldly—ragged beggars, the proletariat.

Karl Jaspers gave a lecture in Rome. He was to speak of mankind's future. The hall was packed. At first the magnet drew normally: his coded language pulled us toward interpretations of ultimate being as material reality and as cipher. He arrived at immortality. We waited for the Marxist view to spring forth. How could he ignore it in these times? He dwelt at length on nuclear catastrophe. And suddenly the hall was full of the Bible. Fabrizio's thesis was on the New Testament. "Let's go, Pietro. I think I'm going to be sick."

We abandoned Jaspers to the satisfied Monsignori, to whom he was surely speaking that night.

"Pietro, do you know Valéry's comment that history never really proves anything? Same for the Bible. Why do they always use the Word of life as an excuse?"

The fire is almost out. Embers flicker and bicker, snapping. My comrades fade into the night, one after another. I stay awake; sleep holds no promise. A familiar landscape surrounds me; as well to meditate it from here. All danger is past. Nothing can reach me now. Odd to tell myself, in this night: *In the sweat of thy face shalt thou eat bread, till thou return unto the ground; for out of it wast thou taken.*

There are only two of us now. The fire is dying. What is this big fellow's name? Is he eighteen? Twenty? He seems no older. A loner. He pays no attention to me. I wish I knew him. His glare revives the embers beneath their ash. A log puffs smoke; it booms gently. Not even that: a soft whistle, and the wood crackles lightly. And the young man? What can he be brooding about?

A faint tug at my heart: I think of a slim collection of poems that I read just before I left Koloso. Jean-Georges Lossier: *Du Plus Loin* (*From the Farthest Corner*). It was my last evening with Howard. I did not know that at the time. I was drinking whiskey and Coca-Cola. The taste of life and happiness. Music soared: Howard had chosen Vivaldi's *Four Seasons*. An encounter with varieties of infinity, perfectly phrased. I had long since ceased to listen closely to that Vivaldi: we were at a crossroads, and politely I respected the right of way. But the strain was followed by a melody; the rising succession of seasons drew me along. They were engraved on my heart. Marveling, I followed on, happy that this ascent was in part thanks to me. I flipped the record, filled the glasses. The turntable jumped off its track. Charming as ever, Howard set about repairing it. That poetry dead for the moment, I needed diversion. On the salon's great table I found Lossier. A Christian poet? They made me nervous. They still make me nervous. . . . I read to discomfit myself, to be surly about the luck that had spoiled our evening.

> *Side by side we bleed*
> *In the same rebellions at dawn.*

I look at the young guerrilla. He is scratching his ear, his gaze still on the heap of cinders. The mosquitoes have lost their fear; they whine close.

> *We have dug up the sands*
> *As far as the deep water*
> *Where the roots of the heart drink.*

He yawned. I was afraid he'd fall asleep on the spot. What will I become without him? He orients me in this night. How I want to understand him! For me he is Christ. To contemplate him is to be briefly rarefied. The mosquitoes: I hope he is not shy of mosquitoes. I hope he would not leave. I wanted to rise and go to him. To suggest some game, to tell him that I love him.

Oh bread of brotherhood
I am nothing without you.

To draw him into the unsayable. To escape this night. A brief vision, a flash: night in the Garden of Gethsemane. The others are asleep. I went on contemplating him. How long can he remain the object of my desires, the Faith of my torment?

He glanced up at me. Modestly I looked away. When I looked up, he glanced at me again. I was afraid. Let him not leave me. How can I keep watch without him? My heart is heavy within me. A warm sweat trickles down my back. The log before me has burst into flames again. The last flickering flames. It too will die. And that will be all.

He has risen, stepped around the hearth and said to me, with a brief wave of the hand, "Good night, comrade."

"Good night."

Alone. An insipid night. They are all gone, even he. *My God, my God, why hast thou forsaken me?* I smiled in embarrassment at my own sickly sentimentality. "My dear Pierre," I told myself, "you have a marked proclivity for your own sex." Shame swept me. I am quite tired. And quite empty. I stood up. To sleep now . . . I stopped, in despair. How long would I struggle tonight, before drowning in sleep?

11

Footsteps. Marching up and down again, hammering painfully. An intrusion, much like this light, much too strong, piercing my closed lids. So I shall never know peace. Never be able to reconcile myself to myself, to marry my actions to my inner life or my presence here to the Gospels. The briefest meditation quickly becomes intolerable. Not because of the void. Mainly because of footsteps pacing. An easy way to drive someone crazy. Surefire. Truss the poor man into a bed and make sure he doesn't sleep or even doze. Then march men up and down in front of him. The footsteps will finish him off for sure. My siesta is no use to me now; I want to run away. And the letter to my bishop embarrasses me now, precisely because it's so like me. It too is a retreat. Writing lets me keep my distance from my conscience: I organize, choose, interpret. The pride in a clear conscience that Saint Augustine mentions . . . I hear my people's travail in those unnerving footsteps, see it in this blinding light. The savage tropical sun. Why is my country thus damned?

Rest period. Tidy terminology. A pretty euphemism to disguise tensions eased and longings satisfied. Is the labor of the spirit easier afterward? Solitude has begun to bore me. I have a hard time resisting Antoinette: those crinkling eyelids. But an interlude with her would only prove that I had broken the last promise of my priesthood. I cannot break it. My vexation is due not so much to the burden of chastity as to the recent simplification of my relations with women. In a parish, in a convent, I should have approached her without fear. Conversation with her would be seen in a different light from one here. The priest functions on the spiritual level. If it asserts itself at all, the intoxication of the flesh is sobered by a context exorcistic because holy.

"Pietro—you won't come visit the nuns of the Holy Child Jesus? Do you have something against them? Last Sunday you never appeared."

I wanted to break with them and had promised myself never to set foot in their convent again. It was silly, because I cheated, groped for reasons, explained myself badly. Fabrizio did not understand.

"Listen, my friend, it's to mortify my soul. I enjoy their company far too much. For a while I want to deny myself that pleasure."

"What are you talking about?"

"The requirements of our trade, Fabrizio. We are not of this world."

"But we have to live in a world where women live too. Woman isn't the incarnation of sin, even if she's the occasion of it sometimes. Ah no, Pietro, once the intent . . ."

And he repeated Sanguinetti's lecture. I thought of a Dutch colleague whose considered opinion it was that this course in morals included some of the hottest pages of pornography he'd ever seen. Fabrizio pleaded with me. I allowed myself to be persuaded, with pleasure, and even forgot the deeper reason for my sulks, a brief article in a small nun's magazine. Celebrating the order's imposing labors in the heart of Africa, they described my country in clichés: the pitiful life of the unfortunate little Negroes; the poor, brutish, filthy savage flinging himself at the feet of the civilizing missionary. The tone had shocked and angered me.

I soon forgot about it, and revisited the nuns with good cheer. Our relaxing conversations, free and easy as we were children of God, resumed each Sunday, brightening the Lord's day and transfiguring me for the week to come. My Spiritual Director, to whom I confided my confusion, said, "No! There is no sin in enjoying their company. You are human and you need them, as they need you. Did Christ flee from woman?" He did not favor Saint Paul and gave him a rough time; and spoke tenderly of the holy women about Christ, the woman of Samaria, Mary Magdalene.

In my normal setting these meetings took on a grand glow; I left relaxed and calm, my ideals secure. But the direction of souls introduced discreet complicities. A priest, I penetrated to the heart of their days and nights. My advice or wishes made their mark on wives and reoriented households, as they might assure privileges to certain dedicated souls. I reigned, I could speak to any woman without embarrassment, and no outraged glance would rebuke me. I was of another world.

It is not the same here. The universe has been desanctified. I'm a soldier like any other. And a male like any other. Regular chats with Antoinette do not direct my mind toward spiritual channels. The distance I keep to preserve virtue sharpens the desire for total communion. I'm afraid I may give in. What would be left of my priesthood if I broke that last promise?

Solitary vices vexed my soul. And have been vexing my soul for some time now. Crises. I wish I could make fun of myself. My own people know nothing of these deviations. Life is simpler and purer. Nature dictates simple answers once for all. Only in my courses on morality did I learn about sexual perversions, before I met them again in the humid confessional. I must ignore them. They are a minor teasing of the spirit. Provided I don't fall when desire returns.

Exhaustion. Sleep comes with vague images, Antoinette's eyelids; the fire reappears in a troubled dream. A mossy, bubbly excitement amid languorous film music: *Viva Maria*. And a parade of Italian Renaissance Venuses. I whirled, whirled, whirled about a dazzling mudpie. The beach. A summer sky, the blue of Lago Maggiore. I whirled and whirled. Fabrizio. Where was Fabrizio? I found his black hat. "Where is my friend, sir?" "He's lunching with Michelangelo in Heaven." The Venuses returned, languid, excessively so. Antoinette's eyelids gleamed, darkened, gleamed again, and died on the white teeth of sirens lost in drunken ecstasy. A song rose, sweet. I knew the words: the cortege of virgins circled the mudpie, pious, singing, "I have sucked milk and honey from his lips and his blood adorns my cheeks." A siren shrieked, just once. I ran toward the lake.

"Pierre, Pierre. Wake up."

"*Deo gratias*," I answered automatically. I woke up.

Antoinette was gazing down at me. "What did you say?"
"An old habit."

"No, you called Gracias. They blew the whistle for lunch a long time ago. We'll be late."

Lunch. The good things in life. I fill my belly without appetite, mutely chanting, live, survive, don't die. It's always sweet potatoes and boiled beans. Energy expended creates a desire to eat. Animals. We have become wild beasts again. Beasts of the sweet potato and the bean. I think back to my dream; it helps me swallow. The song of the virgins. The tune is gone. But the lyrics, yes, they were from the Breviary: *Lac et mel ex eius oris suscepi et sanguis eius ornat genas meas.* On the lips of a Virgin addressing herself to Christ, consolation and husband. A trifle coarse. Time to eat. A taste of rotten earth, lightly sugared. We become ruminants to survive. In silence. Like the beasts of the field.

My stomach is holding up. It's almost a miracle. I used to

suffer heartburn and bellyaches. Had to dose myself. Always medicine, after every meal. It was a ritual. Father Howard swallowed his pills, and I mine. To keep life comfortable. But here, we're only trying to survive. Everything becomes simpler.

I wouldn't have minded something different today. For once a steak with French fries and a salad. After a *potage julienne*. A nice simple lunch that I'd have topped off with an orange soufflé. What could be more normal and ordinary? Priests spend ten times as much on Sunday dinner. If I could only dig into an orange soufflé one more time! They cost next to nothing. It's the dessert I whipped up at Koloso when the electricity was out. A few oranges. They lay rotting all about us. Squeeze out the juice. Heat it, then stir in egg yolks. The parish chickens supplied the eggs. Mix well, add a little sugar, just a bit, with a few spoonfuls of cornstarch. Then a few drops of liqueur, and finally the beaten egg whites. Pour the creamy concoction back into the hollow oranges. Heat them up a trifle—and there's your orange soufflé. How I would likè one! A poor man's dessert. With a steak-fries-salad and a *potage julienne* to start with. Oh, to live it up! Just a bit, before dying.

Sweet potatoes and beans. Beans and sweet potatoes. Not Marx, not Lenin, not Mao requires us to eat so much of either. Why not detach a few riflemen and send them off hunting? We'd have game. The revolution would not be delayed. No. Nobody recommends beans and sweet potatoes out of love for the poor. Not Christ himself. He ate simply but not badly. At home with his friends, Martha, Mary, and Lazarus; he was invited to weddings, as at Cana; feasted now and then with the Pharisees. And then there was the Last Supper.

Even in my childhood home we were poor, but the meals were varied. We ate meat, fish, vegetables. But here it's always the same thing. Tonight, tomorrow at noon, tomorrow night, next day noon and night, next week, next month, next year, in our communist project. A certainty: it will be the same until we're dead. I'm sick at heart.

No, I would not have our meals at all like those pious banquets in the great religious houses. But why does revolution carry the ridiculous to extremes, even structuring our diet?

"Simplicity is purity," Bidoule said.

He thinks he's a deep one. If I liked him at all I might find some profound meaning in that slogan. They're trying too hard to conform. Of course it will backfire. What do the others think about it? They ruminate conscientiously, in silence. I imagine a book: sweet potatoes beans. Raw sweet potatoes and cooked beans.

What I don't understand is, why can't they buy something else when they attack a village or a garrison? They could have had rice at the same cost, for example.

A matter of conformity. One more submission.

The Church submits too. That's what Vatican II was all about. A tactical revision. The world was slipping away. The Church led us by a different path to unfamiliar nourishment. The liturgy is translated into African languages, disclosing the secret of divine communications. The sense of magic dissipates. And the mystery. Christ, our supreme strength, revealed in stark un-ceremonious words, will soon bore us and then disgust us. Unless the revision cancels itself by fully embracing modes of African thought.

In other words: a complete break with occidental Christianity in favor of the seasonal rhythms and esoteric observances of Bantu witch doctors. The rites of hunting and healing, fishing, and building would be reborn then, perhaps transformed. Otherwise the present modifications will deaden the magical powers that Africans responded to. Will platitudinize the message. My colleagues worry about it. They fret and toil so that Christianity will not be reduced to the familiar taste of sweet-potatoes-beans. But do they know that taste?

Oh God, you know my haunting fears! Only you can still understand my sorrow. In my solitude I know that I am with you. That you sustain me. My freedom is only the expression of my love. How would they understand me? They contemplate you and adore you. As I should like to. Aren't they ignoring the atrocious truths of everyday life? They work with pure things. Beautiful things. Can they spare a glance for us who are condemned to the life of animals?

Father Howard lent me Josue de Castro's *The Geopolitics of Hunger*. My corruption began at that moment. About 50 percent of the world's population, one billion four hundred million people almost totally deprived, live on barely 10 percent of the gross international product. The Vietcong taught us more about love of the poor. "From 1960 to 1965 our people, led by the National Liberation Front, annihilated 540,000 enemy dead, wounded and prisoners, including 20,000 Yankee military aggressors. We destroyed or damaged 1,922 military vehicles, and sank or damaged 912 launches and warships. . . . Amid the storms of war, a new life burgeoned in wide areas liberated by our patriotic forces, areas that today comprise over 80% of South Vietnamese territory with a population of 10,000,000. Almost 4,000,000 men and women have joined the organizations and patriotic parties that compose the 'National Liberation Front.' Over 4,000,000 farmers have established mutual aid societies and collective farms. Committees of the Front and committees of Popular Local Administration have been organized at all levels, making the people the true masters of their own lives and their own futures."

Le jour de gloire . . .

Tomorrow. Tomorrow. We might, I might, order orange soufflé. Orange soufflé! No more one-dish boredom! Never. What happiness! We might eat game from time to time, as in the village when I was young. God, forgive me for that letter to my bishop. I betrayed your friends, these poor people. I'm sorry. I wanted to whitewash myself. To be approved and even admired.

I am going to accept my real friends. And the footsteps. Yes, these footsteps driving me crazy. And the goad in the flesh. Take it all upon myself for the tricontinental of the poor.

At dinner I noted again the smell and taste of rotten earth.

Lightly sugared. What's nice about the evening meal is that the silence isn't total. Bidoule reads aloud from a book translated into African languages by the Colonel. The fires of hatred must be nourished, as piety is nourished in the monasteries. He's reading André-Paul Lentin's last book on the tricontinental struggle. We've come a long way from the old notion that African languages are awkward in translating technical terms.

"The imperialist government of the United States can raise an army of 3,000,000 men, blacks among them; disposes of 854 intercontinental Minuteman or Titan III missiles, 544 Polaris missiles, 2,600 nuclear warheads, 50 Polaris-equipped submarines, 1,100 strategic bombers, about 3,500 fighter-bombers with nuclear capability, with an explosive power of 25,000 megatons.

"But they are paper tigers, as Mao stated. Look at Vietnam. . . ."

Do these dizzying statistics intensify the hatred? Yesterday after dinner a comrade came up to me: "What do you think of the United States?"

"Well, I don't know much about the place."

"Are they trying to wipe out the black race?"

"I don't know anything about that. I don't believe they care about race, as long as they can make money."

"Is all that true, what they say about them?"

"What do they say?"

"How rich they are."

He was beginning to bore me. If I could just offend him in a friendly way. "Yes." I said. "Every year they spend five hundred thirty-four million dollars on their dogs. You never saw anything like the luxury their dogs live in. They even have special doctors for them."

I don't give a damn about the United States. We need a scapegoat. We've found it. The innocence of American imperialism in its contemptible single-mindedness: we can hate that. They gauge their hate by the United States. The outrage of unrequited love needs no urging. I live in spiritualized hatred. Don't my own plans prove it? The candor of the American

colleagues I lived with in Rome . . . Why should I hate them?
Ah yes, the death their country sows in the name of capital!

God, teach me to hate my friends. My brothers in your
love—but you know that is not a common denominator.

Our routine dragged out to no purpose. Dinner ended. The
wind was rising. We took a breather before the 7:00 p.m. meeting: after that would come the night's final exercises. Bidoule
appeared. "So, Pierre?"

"You look like a demon. What do you want with me?"

"To say good evening."

"Good evening. Are you all right?"

"All right. You have no regrets? Not still thinking of leaving us?"

"Are you tempting me?"

"Of course not. For goodness' sake, no slogans. I'm talking
to you like a brother. Don't you ever miss the charms and re-
wards of parish life? It must be so calm, so peaceful."

"Yes; but why can't you all believe that I didn't join you for
selfish reasons?"

"We'd like that. But you're a provocateur, aren't you?"

"Do you really think that?"

I thought sadly of the letter to my bishop. A moment of
weakness? Should I confess it? No; no use. I must accept the sad
burden of that momentary treason.

Bidoule was watching me. A man of goodwill. I must learn
to love him. "Suspect you, Pierre? You're old enough to judge
your own responsibilities. I was just talking. No overtones, no
ulterior motives."

I could change nothing by confessing that moment of weakness; change much by reforming myself from this moment on.
Night was falling. The meeting a few minutes from now; and
then the last exercises; and then face to face with myself. Tonight, an uncompromising review of my responsibilities. Revolutionary orthodoxy is also an ideal. A state of grace, with all its
demands.

"Have you American friends, Pierre?"

"Yes."

"Many?"

"Old friends from the university. A fair number, yes."

"Do you hate them?"

"No. I'd like to hate them. I try."

"You ought to hate them. You know that."

"Yes, I know. I ought to."

Hate them. And love Bidoule. Dump Sanguinetti, Howard, Fabrizio, the Americans, in my hatred. Into the mud, my bishop. Yes, but how? Until now my life was theirs. How can I meet them again in Christ? Why meet them again if they were only using Christ?

It's not true. Fabrizio was not merely using Christ. Sanguinetti, perhaps. He suffered visibly because he was only a professor. Howard, unquestionably: his brother owns a great factory that manufactures various oils. Perhaps my bishop, too: he was amazed, he said, when he bought a salt works with his own money. He exports salt. It seems he owns mining stock. For the good of the diocese . . . Perhaps they were using Christ. But Fabrizio? Why should I have to hate him? He isn't even American. I could never hate him. I'd have to hate Christ too. . . .

A Belgian nun, chatting with me about the war in Vietnam, edified me. To annoy her I confided maliciously, "Nasty gossips are saying that the Holy See owns shares in American war industries. Vietnam ought to be quite profitable."

She replied that she was not at all worried about that. "The Pope could send divisions of infantry to Vietnam and it would not shake my faith."

Of course, she's European. That makes a difference. But it would shake *my* faith. Sanguinetti's ambition, the Howard family's profits, my bishop's business dealings. They are recrucifying the poor Nazarene. But Fabrizio?

12

Eternal shortages dispirit our dreary days: austerity becomes asceticism. Thus I expiate the insane pleasure of my mornings; but to remain ascetic is a problem. Austerity may turn to rapacity. I'll be glad of that too, and lose my last scrap of Heaven. How can I continue on this steep slope? Accidents happen suddenly, and I alone will be responsible. The virtue of prudence, which once seemed only a glorification of timidity, fascinates me now. I am terrified of falling; if I do that, my little ball of hatred will swell uncontrollably, and bar me from speaking of Christ.

The courses I give now are killing me. Remote, discouraged, I observe my own assassination. A somewhat macabre scene: the assassin assassinated. A game like the game Charles V played in his retirement: attending his own funeral. Not your everyday amusement. Mine is different: I see myself dying, helpless against the delicate, precise blows that I inflict upon myself. It may seem lugubrious, seeing oneself dead. But much like seeing oneself alive. A beautiful mirror is a luxury for connoisseurs; to reflect oneself, an easy flirtation. So agreeable.

To kill oneself is a bit different. First to plunge the dagger in. Not the heart; that's too quick, too clean. Say a thigh. Then gently, repeatedly, to twist it deep within the flesh, while counting: one . . . two . . . three . . . four . . . up to a hundred. Then to leave it there and pour two soupspoons of alcohol into the bloody gash . . . and leave the dear dagger where it is, deep in the heart of the wound. Take a knife then and begin carefully peeling the toes one after another, yes, peeling them as you would little potatoes. Work slowly; let the spectators see it all. Comment clearly in a confident voice. When the toes are quite peeled and quite bloody, sprinkle salt on them—not too much— just a bit—and not a great pinch of it all at once, but a fine fall of it, as you recite a ringing commemorative poem for the occasion, to accompany the motions of your fingers as they slowly sprinkle the leisurely white cloud.

Back to the thigh: shake a little pepper into the wound, just enough to alter the quality of your pain. Then take an empty bucket. Thrust your left hand into it and with your right hand pour hot water. Slowly, counting. The water should not be excessively hot. That would be too easy, too quick. You must make pain last. The audience will be restless otherwise. At the same time, a drop of water must fall on your head every three seconds: that seems to be a Chinese technique. Every three seconds for ten minutes. Then the rhythm should accelerate every two seconds; ten minutes later, return to the original rhythm. And so on. Make it last.

And a blinding light to stun the eyes, on and off at regular five-minute intervals. Very important, the timing. And during the eyes' five minutes of rest, treat yourself to a luxury: ogle a belly dancer through a carefully filtered rainbow spectrum, and chastely worship the violent desires roused by appropriate music.

The orchestration must be perfect. The agonies must be absolutely simultaneous, and you must absolutely reject any slightest pleasure, either in the torn flesh or in the running account of your own torment.

And for all that big talk, I'm a liar. I must start again. Many

martyrs would accept that for Christ. My assassination is a bit
more delicate. Perhaps I am killing Christ through myself. At
any rate the Church, certainly. Only love for others lets me go
on giving these daily quasi-deicidal courses. Daggers. Knives.
Hot water. Salt. Alcohol. The whole arsenal of the accomplished torturer. I still dare to pray silently before my classes.
And after all, why not?

It was not hard to list my bibliography. I could consult the
Colonel's makeshift library of Marxist classics at will. Out of
sheer laziness I picked up George Cogniot's little book on *Religion
and Science*. The main thing is to succeed, as the Colonel wishes,
in combating the medieval influence of the clergy.

They loved the story of Galileo. I felt undone. Every scandal exposed by Cogniot was a wound reopened in me. All that he
says is true. All of it. But I suffer. . . . How could the Church of
God chain itself so straitly to the past? It is as if she were afraid
of the future—which is nevertheless where eschatological hope
lies. I took revenge on Cogniot and his henchmen. They made
too much fun. How could they not have? They were right to
laugh; it's a sign of good mental health. I finished Cogniot in a
hurry. I was about to proceed to Marx and Engels when by
accident I came upon Jean-Yves Calvez's *La Pensée de Karl Marx*.
I know the book. It was made for me. There is my sweet revenge:
I am lecturing to Marxist militants from the pages of a Jesuit.
Only on religious alienation, and often word for word. But what
am I salvaging, in fact? Almost nothing. I suppress Calvez's
occasional reservations. It's the paradox that amuses me. A Catholic priest is shaping Marxist consciences—better, confirming
them—using the commentaries of an orthodox Jesuit. I find that
at once a little more than beautiful and a little less than sad.

Tricky terrain. Someone may expose the hoax. Of course
there *is* one. Not in my courses or even in Calvez's concept,
which would fit nicely into the dialectic of a certain communist
faction with only a few deletions—the last chapter, for
example—and some afterthoughts. The hoax is in the very nature of my project. I recall Anaximander's dictum, exhumed by

Lefebvre in his *Metaphilosophie:* "Whence things were born, thence must they necessarily die, for they must expiate their injustices and be judged for them according to the laws of the universe."

"That's fascinating stuff," Bidoule told me.

"Oh really?"

"I mean it. A shame you're a priest."

"Why? I'm as much a guerrilla as the others."

"You really believe that?"

Had he pierced my disguise? Why should I lie? No: I am torn because I cannot fully become one of them. Does it show? Doubtless my silences betray me. Does my nervousness show through my cool, withdrawn manner, my dry words and comments? How can I hide a bleeding wound?

"Fabrizio, can a priest be an honest scholar?"

"I believe he can. History tells of many, and there are some alive today."

"But are they scholars because priests, or priests because scholars? Which takes precedence?"

"Obviously the priest takes precedence. It's a hair shirt. I'm sorry for the poor fellows. You see, they can't be——"

The poor fellows, he said. That's it exactly. In the sweet serenity of our Roman residence, when we discussed the eddies and echoes of life, could I have foreseen that I too was condemned to be a battleground? I am one of those poor fellows. Doctor priests, biochemist priests, paleontologist priests—and most of all philosopher priests. We're frustrated by Thomas Aquinas's truths. The traditions of our calling offer only one way out: to the beyond. We are ready to call white black for the greater glory of God. And I can no longer discharge that obligation. It is through weakness? Since I must do violence to myself . . .

"If I'm not a good guerrilla, what do I have to do to become one?" I was making fun of him.

He was cold, rigid, indifferent. Only his small eyes were alive and sparkling. "You state the problem incorrectly. All I asked was if you felt like the others."

He was quite right, this good man. I was trying to be sophistical. Why was he called Bidoule? The name suits him. Some names stick to a man.

"Try to ease up, Pierre. You're insufferable, you know. Always on hot coals, on the defensive every time you open your mouth."

And he walked away. It was true: they aren't persecuting me. The dubious surprised glances of the first week are a thing of the past, or so it seems. And yet I am pursued. Mainly by myself. Remorse? No. I have no regrets, just as I have no sense of having committed evil. I'm only afraid of tumbling off this peak, and my fear springs from the vague but unmistakable feeling that my tumble must come. No hedge, no fence will hold me back. What matters is putting a name to the threat.

I'm helpless in the face of danger, but that has not resulted in mistrust or defiance, even if I've been torturing myself within. Prayer? The psalms have become so much babble. Verses parade sadly past me. I feel sorry for them; yet, against all hope, I force myself to join ranks with them.

Yahweh

Thine arrows stick fast in me, and thy hand presseth me sore. There is no soundness in my flesh because of thine anger; neither is there any rest in my bones because of my sin.

In the Church you must let remorse mature fully if you wish to resume loving. At first, guilt. What did I do? I only read some pages of Calvez's book, a book that any Christian in Europe can find in any bookshop. Well, it's not quite the same here. And the readings I give can differ as intent differs. Are my intentions evil, then?

Dawdling, I lag behind.

Bidoule passes by again. "Coming, Pierre? We're going to have a little fun."

"What's happening?"

"Found a wolf among us." He smiles and adds, "Or a fox. Clever. A tall, quiet, young fellow. Eager and energetic. You know the one I mean?"

"Yes, I know him." I believe I do. The young fellow I yearned toward one night. A traitor in our midst!

"We're going to interrogate him," Bidoule went on. "Nobody can understand how he fooled us for so long."

"Suppose it was a real change of heart?"

"You still believe in conversions, at your age?"

The fool. Conversions *must* be possible.

My own dream is an attempt. Christianity invites us to permanent conversions. That is the whole meaning of the *sursum corda*.

I see him again. The hut is full of light. He's bound hand and foot. Dogs stand watch over him: two guards. German shepherds.

Bidoule wants to have it over and done with. "You going to talk?"

"Yes."

"Why did you come here?"

"Same reason as the others."

"I asked you why."

"Ask the priest why he's here."

Bidoule is furious. The guards clout the prisoner. Stupidity is foreordained. I want to run away but I'm afraid this betrayed soldier will betray me. I stay where I am, and raise no suspicions. I think back to my letter to the bishop. That's behind me; no more of that ever. Forever and ever.

"Talk!" Bidoule is shouting. I witness the trickle of blood welling from the soldier's left nostril. A painful privilege.

"Well?"

"Nothing."

Why doesn't he answer? Why hold out? In the name of what is he laying down his life? In the name of what? I've shut my eyes. A terrible sort of "fun." To pray for him would hardly change matters. It would only be an evasion. His treason is as amateurish as Bidoule's brutal reaction.

Bidoule lights a cigarette. I watch him take a few drags. He's a weakling, I thought; and I was lulled. Suddenly he squats and his right hand snakes out, straight for the soldier's left nostril. I shout, "Cut it out, Bidoule!"

He glares at me.

"That's no use. If he won't talk, your way won't help. Let me do it."

"All right. He's yours."

I cheated. I lied knowingly. I had to clear him to ease his pain. "No, Bidoule. Leave us alone. Yes, tied up, that's your guarantee. Mine too. Yes, of course I'll call you. . . . All right, I'll level with you—I can hit hard when I have to. I used to box. Why? It's a sport like any other. Because I'm a priest? Come on! If a priest can play football or volleyball or tennis, why can't he box? In Rome, obviously. Twice a week." Laughter. "Try to believe it, Bidoule—I had a colleague who was a karate master, a Dutchman." More laughter. "That's a sport like any other too. You want to try a judo throw? Come on, chicken. Right, like that. Ten, fifteen minutes at most. *Ciao.*"

And alone: "Yes indeed, soldier. I'm here for the same reason as you. Almost. Don't sulk like that. I'm not a child, and it doesn't help. Tell me now, will you?"

No. He will not. I rise and leave the hut for a moment. The cool breeze. And the implacable tropical sun, the very emblem of my country. Climatically all is in order. There remains myself. I was afraid that soldier would give me away, and now I have to make him talk. I've even set a time limit. Always projects and plans. What was I hoping for? Fifteen minutes—that's still the future, the unpresent. I turn to him again with no set purpose, blind, indecisive, fearful. I am Maillol's *Pomona*, but without grace or mystery. I go on in.

"Listen, friend, think what you like, but I'm not an execu-

tioner. Not even if I come up dry. Which I don't plan to do. A
fool in just about the same fix as you called me a false priest. It
was silly. I'm more likely a false guerrilla like you." I look him
over. He despises me. "While we're at it I may as well know your
name. Ah! Jacques! I have a friend of the same name. You may
even know him. The Abbe Mitani. He's a bishop? Since when?
Well, good, that's good news. An auxiliary bishop! It's a step up.
He deserves it, doesn't he? Yes indeed, a fine man, a little slow
on the uptake. What? That's a terrible thing to say! You claim
Rome only promotes black priests stupid enough to be manipu-
lated by their white masters? Well, it's possible. It doesn't really
interest me much. But you, my friend Jacques . . . whatever you
say. But what am I going to tell Bidoule? He'll make mincemeat
of you, and for no good reason. You've been here long enough,
you know the rules; they'll execute you. Why let yourself be
beaten black and blue first? Why don't you save yourself a drub-
bing? You're hardly more than a boy. The state, the state, what's
the state anyway? An abstract idea. Well-fed gentlemen in
Charlesville and their popsies and nightclubs and champagne—
that's the state. You know Garbage Girl? Her father died on the
hospital steps. They had no cash to pay his fees in advance. The
state doesn't give a damn about the poor; they can all die, and it
doesn't give a damn, you hear? Think, man, think: you're going
to be killed. Your general or your colonel will hear about it;
Bidoule makes sure executions become hot gossip. Your chief
will hear the news. Do you think that will keep him from his
evening's entertainment? Do what you want. Sort it out for
yourself, but for heaven's sake don't let yourself be beaten to a
pulp for nothing.

"I'm a priest, you know. If you need me, just call."

"Well, Bidoule."

"He's a fool. What did he tell you?"

"We had a friendly talk. He even told me about a school-
mate of mine who's been made a bishop."

"That fat fellow Matani?"

"Right. So what happens?"

"He didn't talk. He's as good as dead." Bidoule is disgusted. He snickers at death habitually. The burden of my own sin is crushing. Did he need me? He seemed at peace when he was with me. I talked freely, even criticized the whole process. I wanted to spare him suffering. He chose it. Had I the right to stop him? After all, other people's free will is not my business. I had offered him my voice so that he could answer as if it were God's. Did he answer? He spoke to me, yes; but did he answer?

The sun is setting and the air is cooler. I'll be reading Calvez to my class after dinner. That irritates me. I wish I could see Jacques, the man-as-good-as-dead. . . .

I did not attend. The ultimate deposition is never very pretty. Just as well to stay where I am. Everything jangles my nerves. Everything. If I only had a detective story . . . There, on my table, a tiny ant. I stop writing, slide my pencil toward it. It backs off. I close off its new path; it turns left. I shove a book that way, and it scoots off again. Do ants panic? A man would have halted for a moment, hopeless, irresolute. Jesus, for example. God that he was, he panicked in the Garden of Gethsemane. He was afraid of suffering. And yet he had every reason to accept his death.

The gallows. Hanged men. Assassins. Fear. All in the same class. I seem to be the center of the world, with everybody staring at me. I return their glances, to transfer my suffering to them. No: I still need their attention. Christ's despair was a sense of the void, the absent watcher. . . .

The Ascension from Mount Carmel to the Holy Fire: John of the Cross also needed the watcher. The night of the senses: how long will I be locked within it? When will I be able to advance toward the Kingdom of Light, to see my own eyes in the eyes of God? To become His; to murmur in tender ecstasy, "Your gaze stamped me with your grace. It was thus that you held me dear. And mine therefore deserved to see what they saw in you, and to adore it." He who shelters in the Most High . . .

Make the light of thy countenance to shine upon me; hover

over me, nearer, nearer. I shall not stir. No, I can no longer
move. I offer myself. You see that I yield myself. Help me. God
vexes me slightly. He breathes me in, and that smacks of do-
mesticity; it is faintly untidy. And that urge toward Him in my
heart of hearts—is it a drive toward nothingness? Toward being,
I believe. I believe—what does that mean now? Well, something. Perhaps the nothingness is myself. Help me, then; do not
abandon me whoever you are; do not leave me numb. If you
want to understand me, perhaps it is I, Elijah, who must come
unto you. You see. I've gone mad. Almost. Am I emerging from
my night? Forward, then! A Marxist is all cold logic. So?

Read Calvez. Drink deep of the monstrous logic that would
end the temporal reign of Christ. I am mad, mad, mad with joy!
Glorify the Lord, O Jerusalem. . . . Topple the rule of the idols
and the reign of idolatrous priests. "The words that I speak unto
you I speak not of myself: but the Father that dwelleth in me, he
doeth the works." Extol his name, O Zion. . . .

"Pierre! Come see!"

Antoinette's voice. The return to reality. I went outside.
An ordinary step or two; I was still braced against sunlight, but
the sun had set.

"That big fellow Jacques killed himself."

"He what?"

"Bidoule just said so. I don't understand. Why should he
kill himself? He was a good tough man."

"Did you know him well?"

A peal of laughter. "Indeed I did. And I loved him well."

"Thanks. I understand."

"Are you jealous?"

Yes, I am. But I cannot admit it. Cannot take revenge.
"And why, if you please, should I be jealous?"

Like having my throat cut. My mouth is dry. A long-ago
dream mysteriously invades my mind. I was in Arab dress. Richly
adorned. Seated before my house, I was smoking a pipe. A dead
cockerel had been hung about my neck. I was happy in the

setting sun. An endless caravan shuffled past; an old housewife surged up from my pipe and asked, "Are you jealous?"

"So what have you been doing that's worth telling me?"

"Exercises. Like every day."

"Are you happy?"

"You bet!" She bursts into laughter. The aroma of life, pervasive, splendid, sets my fancy ablaze. I'm jealous.

"Do you know, Antoinette, I'm dying of jealousy."

13

A HOLIDAY SUN. FLAGRANT, indiscreet. But soon, twilight. Finally an end to this indecent excess of blinding light. And with the coming of night, some relaxation, some relief from my solitude. Even if it is only fugitive, it distracts me from the ruthless and demanding inner fire. In it I can awkwardly—timid, fearful, terrified—prepare myself for another day.

Games of hide-and-seek in the forest are rather ridiculous. Sanguinetti used to say that any talent comprised some small ridiculous element to be transcended. So the death dogging my footsteps might, my God, resemble love slightly. I believed that to be a good man I must surrender my rights. Will these military drills, by reducing me to the ridiculous, grant me the desired capacity for love? *We are all sinners.* In Saint Paul's brutality I see the extent of the disaster. It saves me temporarily by affirming my moral solidarity with my comrades, and the good intentions that their bad faith hatches. So why must I go on hiding the light within me? Is that the condition of my calvary?

So be it. On parallel planes. Or even successive. Forget

language. After all, it bores me. The senses. And this much is true: any communication must transcend the immediacy of solidarity, must be mediated by ideological and economic connections. And there the senses reappear. No use giving in to words. My damnation might shed its burden of love.

I choose the blinding sun. Once.

The races and obstacle courses through the trees have given me a backache. A sign. The body suffered in God's service, the stigma appears between the decision and the painful intoxication of sanctity desanctified by hard work. The worker-priests made me feel the gulf.

"That's sacrilege," Fabrizio asked me, "isn't it?"

"Their intent, even as they shock the middle classes, is to bear witness before these same good people."

"And what does that mean?"

"The average worker or peasant will never be entirely convinced. The worker-priest is the incarnation of a concrete symbol, yes, lifelike but not a reality."

"There's sacrilege, Pietro. A *te numquam separari permittas*— that's our prayer. The Church gives us the means and the historical structures. The priesthood is a nobility. These worker-priests are betraying something. I think of Christ, and of all those burdened and troubled by his truths: *Et jam cum illo non ambulant.*"

The beauty of Scripture is that it supports all points of view. So the scandal of the worker-priests can be reduced to a kind of hoax. The same that has unbalanced me. That's why the newspapers gave them so much space. They needed just men, even for filler. I know that I am far from being that, though I resemble them a bit in my private gloom. For the moment, only my aching back matters. It was the same yesterday. And will probably be the same tomorrow.

One, two, three, go! It was a five-hundred-meter race through the brush as far as a hillock. We snaked through. Yes, we were snakes, exercising before we struck. Be as the serpent . . . but the analogy terrifies me.

. . . two, three, go! The sergeant takes it all in from the top of a termite hill. With a grim eye he follows the animals learning to do evil. We must be pure snake. Like them in all things: unconscious innocence, increasing agility in adversity, a naturally shifty malice in self-defense.

One, two, three, go! . . . two, three, go! And back. We have to beat our old record each time. The sun, the heat, the sweat. I swim along, my thought fragmented, my soul afflicted, my eyes soaking up blood. The sweat on my arms can't even form drops; it oozes out and streaks down the arm immediately. Scrub is everywhere, scratching, stinging. Words swarm into me. I would at least like to name these living things I roll among, name them in my mother tongue, but I don't know the right words. I give names to another world: the world of mummulaires and fetuques, and clematis like silver buttons. The houques and the cuscutes, grasses like Patagonians, like cats, like poor men, even like pearls, are there any here? Signs of a mind demented. If only I could name the causes of my present torment, I would feel much enchanted. Yes. What a reward! Sad, but at least I'd know what had wounded me.

One, two, three, go! After the anguish prophesied by the one and two comes a dreadful torment: three. . . . To plunge into the swarm of needles, splinters, green leaves that fear makes dangerous.

How pleasant, the recreation period with its lessons in knife play! A necessity. Learn how to cut an enemy throat in a dozen different ways, from any position. A sweet mess!

I'm not even disgusted now. I accept these new techniques that may produce another dimension of charismata. My country's guilty political and social structures justify this new art. I remember the title of a book I glimpsed a few years ago on the Via Veneto. *On Assassination as One of the Fine Arts.* I'd like to read it. At the time, the title made me smile. My sleek knife, which I have learned to love, which is joined to me as if by a bond, calms my temptations. Like a breviary. I twist in the same fever, the same meditation, racking my brain, searching my soul, seeking signs. Will my priesthood reaffirm itself in the end?

Ah God, no, this kind of material beauty is not the fruit of a degeneration, not even of a demoralization. It seeks to herald a new life for men of goodwill. I'm all for that life. So I must accept and love this cortege of cold and holy hatred. The bitterness that occasionally swells behind my eyes is only an indication of some fleeting inner crisis, of some temptation to abandon you, my God. I must get used to it; must go so far as to love the taste of blood. The blood of your promise.

Am I going to die? The burden of that promise!

My grandmother: "Landu, there are signs that predict death. Alone beneath the moon, call upon your ancestors. Or before a fire if there is no moon. Immolate a white hen for your ancestors while you recite their litany. Let this hen be prepared forthwith. Offer it as food for the sick; even the least slice of the immolated bird. Then set one of its feathers in a milk can. Before dawn the next day, look at it: if the feather is dry, then the ancestors demand this living soul."

Certainly, I'm all for it. Only I'm not sick. I don't even plan to be. It's my heart, my spirit. Why can't I perform the exorcism myself? Lose myself?

One, two, three, go! One, two . . . go! A spell falls upon me. One of Fabrizio's weaknesses grips me. Where was it? Venice or Assisi? Yes, Assisi. One evening. Heat. Sweat. Brain fag. Conjuring up the Seven. A casual notion. "It's dangerous, Fabrizio." No matter. To liberate myself. Positive thinking won't do it this time. There's too wide a gap between me and my conscience. Marxist clarity does not tolerate this sort of fantasy. Mocking, I see myself perform, smiling as the one, two, three, go! burst out, charging into thickets that for the moment do not exist.

In the name of Michael, may Jehovah command you and send you far from here, Chavajoth!

In the name of Gabriel, may Adonai command you and send you far from here, Belial!

In the name of Raphael, vanish before Elchim, Sahabiel!

By Samael, Zabaoth and in the name of Elohim Gibor, get thee hence, Adrameleck!

By Zachariel and Sachiel, Meleck, obey Elvah and Samgabiel!

In the divine and human name of Shaddai and by the sign of the Pentagram that I hold in my right hand, in the name of the angel Anael by the power of Adam and Eve, who are Iiotchavah, get thee hence. Lilith: leave us in peace, Nahemah!

By the holy Elohim and the names of the demons Cashiel, Schaltiel, Aphiel and Zarahiel, by the command of Orifiel, turn away from us, Moloch! We shall offer you no children to devour.

"Ah, Pietro," Fabrizio said, "we *must* live out of society. Survive by links and connections, and for that, maintain a certain flexibility of expression. There lies salvation. Think of Christ, who to save us offered parables."

"And how can we accept the peace of a sheltered life if we are the salt of the earth?"

"My friend: he said that he came to confirm the Prophets and the Law, not abolish them. Where do they begin? Christ passed them to us alive and useful. And since then?"

Lost in the sensual languor of a beautiful summer. Gazing at the sky, amid a crowd. Christ reappeared to me, the eternal enigma, in the prestigious Byzantine painting. He triumphs in the unctuous climate of churches. There, it is easy to be Perfection. I must make him known without diminishing the mysteries or denying history. But my own heart?

"Pierre: you've read your Karl Barth? You'll find ideas there that the old woman who was almost my mother at the hospice taught me. We who have not glimpsed the Lord are the happy ones. We can live his life in the myths that history ordains— sacred and profane history. We interpret them. That's a lot easier, isn't it?"

The weather was kind; we took these wonderful liberties beneath a flat blue sky. It was the discreet outward sign of an established Truth. But right now I must rest my aching back.

That is far more important. My breath, in rhythm with eternity for over twenty years, rebels at these strenuous exercises intended to transform both today's tempo and eternity's to instant love. "Landu, it is time you drank deeply of the wisdom of your ancestors."

I entered the great seminary. Yet my uncle was waiting to introduce me to my past. How to combine two upbringings? The prospect forced me to cut short my last holiday with my family. I recalled only too vividly the taste of goat's blood, which I had drunk before. Discouraging. I had fled, refusing to compromise myself. Had I not abjured Satan and his works?

"You can leave us," said my uncle. "Wherever you go and whatever you become, something in you will be missing, Landu. You have rejected the life of your own people."

It was not even a curse. My back simply made me aware of my fatigue. There was nothing "missing"; rather, something atrocious had been added. An empty core—yet full of the horror of emptiness. Could the annihilation of the spirit be the hoped-for miracle?

One . . . two . . . three . . . go. The strength to destroy. Possessed by existence. The face of the present. Go! I was crawling—at best. The burden and attraction of affinities is a beautiful thing; they restore the depleted outlook. I was crawling, trying to make as little noise as possible, knife in hand. A rude pleasure began to warm my heart. Another five yards, maybe less; I'll make it; I may be the first across the line. The others can't catch up. Practice. My personal technique. Instead of driving forward on my knees, I proceed on tiptoe. With my back arched like a fat sassy cat's and my hands parting the brush. At the slightest sound I drop to my elbows and knees. I peer about; I lie prone. I'll finish the course for sure. I'll make it. Another five yards? The termite hill can't be much farther. Thank you, God, for helping me to . . .

"Comrade 134, report to camp."

Garbage Girl's voice. A small voice, somehow already ossified. At her age! Wait: that's me, 134. I stand up. The sergeant watches me leave, impassive. I'd hoped for a word of praise for my unfinished performance. Nothing. He watches, stony. I didn't make it.

"Suzanne—who's sent for me?"

"Bidoule. The Colonel's away. Bidoule's in charge."

Since the end of our mission she's recovered her sharp tongue and cold manner. That hurt me. I was hoping I'd understood her somewhat, and I was expecting a warmer friendship.

"Why's he sending for me now? It's against the rules."

"Yes. It must be important."

She fell silent. Now my head aches. I shake it to shoo a fly, and I look closely at Garbage Girl. I hear her regular footsteps, shorter than my own, crushing the dry leaves. I look at her again. Fear steals into me. A need for friendship grows.

She understands. "Pierre: I know what my errand means. Whenever they send for a man this way, in the end they shoot him. Why? A major infraction. Unless disaster's already struck. That would explain the Colonel's long absence."

A major infraction or a general disaster? The letter to my bishop comes to mind immediately. Surely an infraction. Was that it? No, impossible. Why would they have waited a week? Easy does it, Pierre. Think what you can do for your comrades. Disaster has struck. The long night will begin again. The peace of mindless violence. Love as a way of life.

I am quite calm.

It could not have been that silly letter. My messenger was trustworthy. If not, he would have denounced me long since, for the questions I asked every time he came to the camp.

Fear vanished. I let myself appreciate the beauty of the tree trunks along my path. That's valuable wood, I said to myself. If we ever get this country reorganized, there's a natural resource to exploit.

Bidoule is sitting on the Colonel's footstool. That's life. Men come and go. Instruments, means, tools. We deceive our-

selves that we are the users of tools, when it is we who serve
them. Howard told me that. No instrument is necessary to the
glory of Christ. I saw the Via Veneto again. Dummies in a show
window, a world of their own. Languorous in their poses, exciting and unattractive, they mock us. "What do you think of these
mannequins, Fabrizio?"

"They're too beautiful, Pierre. Too alive. An occasion of
sin." Offered to the living passions of strollers passing their win-
dows, the mannequins gratified desire. They were beyond man's
control. Complacent in their marmoreal purity, splendidly
dressed, they became another world, instead of useful objects.
"They are the incarnation of evil; sin itself."

Man, the instrument of sin. Or of a revolution. One day the
Colonel would be gone.

A suspicion is born suddenly. I stamp it out. I remember the
Colonel saying: "A bullet in the back of the head. Mostly likely
fired by a comrade." It was only a suspicion. Feathery, followed
by a contraction of the heart. I will have survived! Then I have
failed. I must begin again.

Impatiently I watch Bidoule. Scripture rushed to my mind: . . . a
pillar in the temple of my God, and he shall go no more out . . .
a lamb . . . sin no more, lest a worse thing come unto thee. But
God! I preached peace and goodwill among men. A memory of
the Colonel: "Attitudes—that is the significance of words."

That's why Bidoule disappointed me. He seemed drunk. His
gaze flitted to the peony. He'd been smoking hemp, the fool; if
we have to remake the country with men like that . . . ! I sat
facing him, discouraged. To Bidoule, my presence in the camp
was a mortal threat. Without assuming some offense, how could
he set the times aright? I missed the Colonel. What had become
of him? Bidoule's fetid breath stank in my nostrils. "We need
you, Pierre," he said. "You'll have to sign something."

"Why?" I thought of the Colonel; perhaps it was for him.
"Of course I will."

Yes, of course. After the letter to my bishop, I was serene. They knew my feelings at the bishopric. If the letter was a small treason to my life here, so much the worse, as long as it expressed some part of my love. A soldier set a paper before me, folded four ways. I signed it without a second thought.

The essential is to hold out here, God. As long as possible. Have I betrayed you? No. Signing, I did not forget the mental reservation, in case the hidden text contradicted the verities of my faith. I thought of Sanguinetti with affection. I betrayed neither my teachers nor their teachings.

"You're a real bastard," Bidoule said. In a voice rich with hate he repeated, "A bastard."

All I could see was his eyes, exaggeratedly dilated. "And why is that?" I asked politely.

The only answer was a sharp blow from the soldier beside me. Another. A third. They bashed at my head; it will burst, I thought, desperate. My ears hummed. And there in the distance Bidoule stared at me unblinking. Was he smiling? I tried to make him out. The question took on great importance for me. Was he smiling? Hammer blows. His smile. Hammer blows on my skull . . .

I came swimming up out of it. Fearfully. My head . . . had not burst. I sucked in healing air. The sea, yes, the sweet fresh feel of the open sea. Now my eyes focused on Bidoule. No, he was not smiling. Had he been?

"We got the letter meant for your boss."

"For my bishop?"

"Yes, for your bishop, if you prefer."

Then I understood. The duplicity was much in the Colonel's style. He had made use of that little villager. Living outside the camp, the little fellow was the only one who could break through my defenses, talking to me of my soul's love. Crazy me. Like a schoolboy. I was sorry about the second half of the letter. A victory for my religious sentimentality. Well, it was all the same now. I wanted to meditate on Christ crucified, but the stupidity of my situation removed me too far from that. It receded. . . .

"Do you know the fate we reserve for traitors?"

"Yes."

Bidoule burst into laughter. "Someone show him a copy of the letter he just signed."

My head ached. The Italian lakes. Cool air. My calm returned, and I accepted my defeat as a gift. I would pay the price. That was customary. Peace. Finally peace rose within me, miraculous, empty, unconditional, based on nothing. I considered myself almost unlucky to be enjoying it so late in the game. So late . . .

"And what is the very reverend Father Landu thinking about?" asked Bidoule.

"Father Landu is thinking," I said, rather amused, "that you ought to see a psychiatrist, and that he would recommend one with pleasure."

I was making judgments again. As before. In Rome, at Koloso. A dream had ended. I saw clearly: good, evil. It was a clean break. I was shedding the weight of my existence among these people. It seemed impossible. So easily! Bidoule's fat laugh filled the hut. I scanned the copy of the letter I had just signed. It was typed. It was effective. Bidoule was a tough one. And a good one—good for my weaknesses. He was trying to save me.

I have just understood what you and yours stand for. I can no longer tell you anything more than this: your rule is ended. I regret and renounce the life I have lived among you. Henceforth faith in my people's revolution will be my aim and my whole purpose in life. To suppress exploitation in all its forms, particularly the religious kind, will be my life's work. My comrades and I are going to drain the huge abscess that is the Church in this country.

Hoping to see you again shortly, I remain, Monsignor, your very sincere

It was well done. Bidoule or the Colonel? Why was the Colonel not here? In its cold logic the letter followed a natural

line of development. The same that I would have followed, if not
for certain scruples. It was a perfect sequel to the revolt that had
made me leave Koloso without my superiors' permission. With
my signature scrawled across the original, my bridges were
burned. A second death. In fact, my comrades were helping me
not to deny the impulse that had led me here. Should I be
grateful to them? They were after all preventing me from betraying the faith of the poor. But doesn't my apostasy cut me off from
the Mystical Body? I try to remember the promise of my death.
When the Colonel returned, I would be executed, Bidoule had
said. "He gave you a week to recant. He would have let it pass.
I tried to help you. You turned me down every time."

Bidoule is watching me now. His pity makes me uneasy. He
says in French "*vous*" and not "*tu*." Humiliation was digging a
breach between us. The lid has been raised, the steam is escap-
ing. It was so clear, so simple. My presence in this camp was, yes,
a vain attempt to find freedom.

I am bound hand and foot to the myths of a spiritual world.
Wholly at the mercy of a vision embedded in my blood and
bones. Sooner or later I would have betrayed. Did I not betray at
the moment I entered the major seminary? My uncle's words will
dog me always: "You rejected life among your own." Examined
closely, what does that mean?

"You're just a nothing, Pierre."

Bidoule was right. I could taste my own bitter saliva. The
smell of my blood. Like a fool I thought I was a man misunderstood. And yet it is all quite clear. Fated to treason. No, not
possible! Since the Catholic priesthood is never tainted by
desertion— It's a hothouse, isn't it? A balanced suffering wit-
nessed to my sincerity— It was the prick of a guilty conscience.
So what? I worked faithfully, but I'm only human— After the
renunciation. In the absence of your own people! God is one in
all his revelations— Why were you so interested in sorcery; did
you ever renounce your customs? The Church is universal, and
Catholicism answers all calls— By assimilation. What are you? Is

a European priest any different from you? My present contradiction . . . Is it any different from the contradictions of a European priest torn between his Christianity and a Marxism modified to ease his conscience?

I inhale the odor of earth. The sun will not rise again. Misunderstood. No, it is too easy to be misunderstood. Everybody is misunderstood, like the slogans we live by. A shit! I am only a vile shit. My filthy conscience. I was dreaming; the future would do me justice; Pierre Landu, priest and martyr.

Martyr in what cause? To Christianity I have long been a renegade. To the partisans, just a nothing, a traitor whose faith they guaranteed by a letter to his bishop. Helpless; the fear of death is expanding in my belly. I smile to save face.

"Are you making fun of us?" Bidoule was furious.

"No, of course not."

Two hands closed on my throat. I was suffocating. Blows slammed at my head. Bludgeons. A bulldozer. Military marches on the Piazza. A vast din. I begged.

14

AND SO ALL SEEMED OVER. THE
rapture of the cross: just another insanity. I am one of the nice
gentiles. My vocation, and I knew this, was treason. Does every
priest trail the odor of treachery? The incompatibility of diverse
kingdoms.

Fabrizio once told me, "Purity is always corrupted by inten-
tion. There is always evil in the intent." The justice of redemption: a slogan. The fault was not in my stars, but in myself: all
had come upon me as a consequence of my saving grace.

The cage was dank, my poky little filthy hole. My sky poured
down through a drainpipe. Strait is the gate. Ah, frankly it was
all the same to me. A smattering of psychology was all you
needed to set your terms of reference. The anguish of death?
Another slogan. I felt nothing yet but the emptiness in my soul.
A yawning void. Luckily I could fall back on memories. Atten-
uated, perhaps, but they could not be faked. My promised death
seemed only one more blind swerve in the fog. Would I be at
peace afterward? I declined to go on inventing possibilities. My

overimaginative, artificial constructions might drive me, as before, into bitterness rather than the joys of childhood and divine intimacy. To be shot! And afterward? A downward spiral.

A peace . . . not at all unpleasant. I had sinned: If I love God, why have I deprived men of his glory? No, no more memories to tear me apart. I had accepted a provisional eternity; I would revive it, stark but indefinable. It is a fine thing to see one's end come. An agonizing end blurs any clear view of the historical tapestry we call life. Sickness, decrepitude. I shall die on my feet, in glory, master of my own past. In the unreal but realistic light of a Caravaggio. A finished composition against a dark background, so that a diffuse life, between light and shadow, surges forth. A masterpiece . . . to love life is enough.

Daylight had come. My mind turned to the Colonel. Rain was falling. Low black clouds had gathered over the camp during the night: it was still dark in my cage. Rain trickled, puddles grew. I had spent the night squatting, unthinking, doubtless happy. The ache in my legs restored me to the day and the dim light. A portentous day, muggy, heavy rain. I raised my body, trying to stand; the wet rope that bound my feet tripped me down again. I peered at my bare feet and dreamed about the carefree life of the well shod. Happy, set free. I supposed that my moments were numbered—when all was said and done, dismal, boring, dull moments. The impending abyss would be a definitive deliverance. I concentrated tenderly on that. The break at last, and with all this rain . . . God seemed to have drowned himself in it.

Weariness. I considered my wounds. A sharp pain in my back hurt like hell. Why do we say hurt like hell? I almost smiled. It was rather wonderful to note that I was still alive. Set conundrums about language, and solve them with appropriate sarcasm—that was life. I had time. Edgy? Not really, now now. I should have been wishing for life and sunlight. It would have cost me nothing. But I composed myself instead for the last liberating wait. Bound and chained, I could mimic life by twisting and turning. But my immobility was preparation for peace and order. I preferred it to all possible loves.

The damp silence reeked: the stink of wet earth, soiled by one fearful prisoner after another.

"Twelve hours at most," Bidoule had told me. "It will happen then. The shack is a bit dirty. But you'll have more to think about than bad smells."

The bad smells provoked meditation, or more exactly attempts at meditation. On that level too I was bound hand and foot. Launched toward heaven, my prayer returned implacably to this universe, where I was hugging myself, my limbs aching. All I could feel was my own weight and the call of time, which would put an end to my abomination.

"Pietro, my friend: Would you like to be a martyr some day?"

"It is a good thing to die witnessing, Fabrizio."

"I'd like that too. Suffering accepted, in dignity and gallantry, heroically for Christ's sake. I envy the martyrs. They go to their death chanting the Lord's praises. To die in your bed is foul. I saw an old bishop. . . ."

Martyrdom! I'm going to die because I betrayed my comrades. Sincerely and earnestly they will execute me, erasing my treason, that cheerful letter. So I shall die without betraying my only true love. Martyrdom! Another word. Just another word. I was drunk; at any rate fuddled by the thick reek of urine and feces in this black hole.

I forced myself to call out. Life insisted. "Hey! Hey!"

Two guards barred the door immediately. With the unblinking gaze of carnivores. I told myself that if I moved or called out again, they would flay me. Die, yes; but not suffer. Humbly I said, "It's nothing. My back hurts badly."

They exchanged uncertain glances. The larger of them went back to his sentry's march in the rain, to-ing and fro-ing outside the doorway. The other one leaned against the jamb and just observed me. The big one muttered and grumbled as he marched

from one end of the hut to the other. I felt life surge into me: a
human voice. How fine! Now they were not wild beasts. The
little one was still watching me. I cleared my throat; and again;
humbly offered him a glance; let him see my helplessness, my
submission. A simple gesture on his part would have eased my
mind. I was afraid they'd beat me. I forced an unhappy smile. My
back to the wall, juices welled up in me, strong, insistent, while
I sweated in fear. "Comrade," I ventured.

"I am not your comrade now. And never was."

A river was rising. The regular rhythm of the rain. They
would beat me again. Panic. I felt the blows in advance. They
loved whacking the head. Talk to them. "You're a veteran here?"

"So. Priest is scared."

"Yes, I'm scared. You're not going to beat me, are you?"

"Oh yes. A priest killed my mother," he said, full of hate.

"No. That can't be true. A priest may not kill. Will never
kill. Above all a woman."

"And you've done no killing here?"

"But I was on your side."

"That's why you're in here. A priest, on our side!"

His face was impassive. He came forward, approached me
calmly. He is not happy. Resentment fills me. What have I done
to him? Nothing; I have done nothing to him. My vision blurred.
I waited for a blow to the head. I heard him say to the big one,
"I'm going to work him over a little, the priest."

"Don't damage the goods too much. We need him alive
later to shoot him."

The bash came, to my head. It was brutal. He took another
hard shot. The ache in my limbs flared up, sharp and insistent.
In the next cell someone was banging on the wall; it echoed in
my head. A violent smash to the lower back made me puke. He
stood there watching me. "What do you think you are, a martyr?"

I glared back at him. I hated him. I wanted revenge. How?
No: forgive him. But would forgiveness be anything more than

an admission of impotence? Yet what could I do, if not forgive him, and so recover a certain peace in my own soul?

"You think they'll canonize you?"

I turned away; my soul seethed with hatred. Sheer physical pain made me understand the need to forgive. True, God had commanded it. But isn't that because it's healthier? The desire for revenge is hazardous to your health.

"Come and look at this," he shouted. "The priest is crying! How do you like that?"

Prayer: I needed to pray. To forget my fall from grace. I tried. The gap widened almost visibly. God is always too far off. . . .

You bloody fool! You know it doesn't do a damn bit of good! An immense message echoed in my head, drowning the divine abandon. A blood-red word, the blood my own. There I was, my face bloody, almost scarred like this other fellow's. He was myself, that other fellow. And I with an enormous placard hanging about my neck. Appropriate, for a man condemned to death. What could I do about it? After all, it was true: Pierre Landu, priest and traitor. That was suitable. That was fair enough. Yes, yes, but for pity's sake, peace. I agree, yes, I am a traitor. Yes, yes, whatever you want, whatever you want. For pity's sake, mercy on a traitor.

"Your people will miss you," my uncle had said, over ten years before; I refused the rites of initiation. What did he mean? It was I who missed them. Could that be the curse they laid upon me? The litany rose in me, gently at first, then deafening and dazzling, abolishing all thought: "Wait for the moment when our ancients descend. Your head will be aflame, your throat will be bursting, your belly will gape open, and your feet will be broken. Wait for the moment when our ancients descend." Well, they had descended. And all I had to defend myself against Africa was a barren, rationalized faith.

A volley of submachine gun fire woke me. I was ashamed of my moaning and groaning. Had the dikes burst? Life flowed back into me with the grenades and rifle fire sweeping the camp. In the rain. Nothing new and different about this: but it was working. Sharp cries rang out: "Soldiers!" "Evacuate the camp!" "Hurry up, you fools!" "Sons of bitches!"

Antoinette rushed up to me: "Quick, Pierre. Government troops." It was their turn to win a battle or two. Hidden in a clump of brush, we observed an abrupt turn of history. A dream of love was ending. Garbage Girl came into view. She was in the grasp of two soldiers. She was screaming and gesticulating: "Garbage, garbage, garbage!" They were kicking her. It was not funny or even shocking. Ridiculous perhaps. They shot her at point-blank range. Perfect. In the natural order of events. A classic mopping-up operation. Clean sweep. The kingdom of God is safe, I thought.

A wall is crumbling away. I can't even say it's a result of my fall. Powerless, I watch my successive dreams dissolve, suffering a pain I don't even want to hide. I even understand that I am becoming less exigent, softer. This time my defeat seems to reconcile me with the peaceful sadness of Limbo. I understand my black colleagues who furnish their lives carefully, ignoring any suggestion that their mission is absurd.

The odor of alcohol and ether. When I awoke in this hospital bed, Jacques Matani, auxiliary bishop of the diocese for some time now, greeted me with his ineffable Pepsodent smile. He exuded honeyed words. I prefer the more aggressive stench of my medications.

"You've returned from afar, Pierre."

"Yes."

Farther than he knew. I had been driven by specific imperatives, and had made my own way. He was probably referring to my coma. As if that were important. He simpered, and lavished charm upon me. All that clerical sweet talk to win me back! Strayed lamb that I was. Except that he had the effect on me of an old rake who, for one moment of pure pleasure, would expose himself to a budding adolescent. Between what I had wanted to be and what he personified, there was a considerable gulf. With his artless indiscretion Monsignor the auxiliary bishop bore the burden of the only real treason, to my way of thinking: not knowing that he was a divided soul.

"How do you feel, my poor Pierre?"

His solicitude was maddening. I thought of Antoinette and felt a bitter smile curve my lips. I'd been like him in my time. "Poor Pierre." Always catchphrases, the required clichés, empty. Which side was I on? A distant refrain came to me out of no-where: "Things are tough all over." To sleep, to close my eyes against this portrait of a world so complacent in the sanctimo-nious good faith of emasculated, thickheaded priests wandering innocently against a ghastly white background.

"The Bishop cannot come himself, Pierre. He is exception-ally busy. He almost had to come to blows with them to keep the police from harassing you. And you must understand, my poor friend, after what . . ."

Come to blows. I know just how. One phone call. At the most, one social call. Of course. I understood. After what I had done. That was logical. He could not come himself. Not right now. I was from somewhere else. He stood apart from me. For-tunately, in my solitude I still had heaven. So silent. The vio-lence of my need endeared heaven to me all the more—this empty heaven.

"Yes. It was very good of you to come, Jacques. Thank you."

That was a lie. I was cheating. They were drawing me back, sucking me in. I would relearn the mannerisms of the caste, the required idiom of the ministry. And then I would make my confession. A sincere repentance. A brave act of contrition. The Bishop would embrace me, of course. . . . I can't do it. And above all, I don't want to do it. But he was jubilant. Good old Jacques: a child.

"You know, the greenhouse priest is my secretary. I have a

secretary now. A wonderful chap. He installed an electric bell for me; I push a button on my desk and a sign lights up on the door: 'Come in' or 'Please wait.' Fantastic, isn't it? Don't fidget like that. You'll make yourself worse."

Stupidity is often a blessing, I reminded myself. I raised my pillow a bit. The motion revived my pain. My groans spared me a moment of his chatter. He was talking away, his silliness culminating in a funny face. As if he were making spiritual jokes. Maybe he was. . . .

"That reminds me, Pierre—do you know our new gardener? You'll have to thank him. A devil of a fellow, but a heart of gold. He found you in the parish flower beds. . . ."

I listened carefully. Something subtle: his last "you" was a "*vous.*" They found more than me alone. A foolish embarrassment kept me from asking the only important question. It burned on my lips. He seemed even more embarrassed than I. Dear God, just let him not stop talking.

He finished in the proper bitter tone: "She was dead. You were in a coma."

Who could help me? The Christ of the Deposition had a sorrowing mother in attendance. I could only live out my torment alone. Monsignor is embarrassed. He is staring at the remains of my breakfast on the night table: a cup, in it a few last drops of the coffee that resurrected me; an open jar of jam; a slice of bread I've barely nibbled. A napkin, a knife, a dirty fork. My new status symbols. I was weeping. There were footfalls in the hallway. Jacques stepped to the sink to close the tap firmly; it was dripping. I had a sudden vision of the unreal beauty of Michelangelo's *Pietà*. So that too was only myth, a message as interpreted by an era. That too! Even that was not firmly embedded in an eternity of truth. Slowly Antoinette's death was sinking in. I tried to recall her face. I could only remember a few things she had said in the camp—trite, empty out of context. Meager enough memories. I wanted to pray for her. I closed my eyes. I saw an infinity of black rifle muzzles bearing on my forehead.

Happy woman. Her body restored to the earth and her spirit outside time. Our flight through the forest was a series of frozen images. The rattle of submachine guns had ceased. Prone on the grass, we had watched soldiers swarm over the camp, destroy the barracks and the tamped earth buildings. The ground must have been strewn with corpses. Antoinette was choking back sobs. . . . For hours we crawled through the grass. A chill sensuality, provoked by the odor of Antoinette's sweat, rose to my head. But the possibility of poisonous snakes subdued the flesh and reminded my soul of the brand on my forehead.

Dawn overtook us in a small valley. With sunrise the poetry died. Forever.

"What do you plan to do, Antoinette?"

"Nothing. I don't know."

"Your family, relatives, people—where are they?"

"I don't know. I think they were all killed."

A blessing. She had volunteered for a fighting unit. Unconditionally. No way back. Burned all her bridges. In the name of the law she had been discharged. On the spot she became nothing. All I had to do, on the other hand, was to be—or even play—the prodigal son. Yes, that was all. A statement from my past, I couldn't tell just where or when, came back to me: "To keep your place beside the hospitable throne, they asked only that you pretend to forget."

Forget? The return to a just path? Which just path?

"We'll find something, Antoinette."

Antoinette's exhaustion and sobs were a kind of calvary too. Did we share the same hopes? That made no difference. I could not rise above revenge; I was too bitter at the emptiness of freedom. They consider themselves just and decent. They never run the slightest risk. It's not hard to live like that. All you do is go along. I had agreed this once to become an instrument of living hate. But was I still strong enough to hate, or only to blaspheme? To fight over a yes or a no—wasn't that trivializing the power of hatred? I agreed to judge before I was judged— And the joyous truths? But I had none ever, except God— Which God? The God of Abraham, Isaac, and Jacob— And he taught you hatred? Since that is the only expression of love I'm still capable of— And the truth of Virtue? Virtue does not and cannot exist except in action— Heretical, don't you think? Me? Yes, you, Pierre, heretical. You're a heretic, a renegade, a traitor. . . .

I was smiling. It was just like Joan of Arc. Such is the intelligence of the world I live in! All has been foreseen. Virtues as well as vices. They have been labeled once for all. They can exist only as described and defined. What becomes of God among all those words?

By nightfall we were on the Bishop's farmland. His people would show me pity, which would revive my hate. I must stoop even lower, and beg for pity so that the Kingdom of God . . . Rifle fire welcomed us. Antoinette fell shouting my name. They recognized me, I thought. Monsignor surely got Bidoule's letter. I dived for cover at the first volley. More shots rang out. But I cared only about the fire raging in my belly.

Now I looked at Jacques. He turned away immediately. What was he looking at, through the window? His thick lips stirred. So he could pray that easily! For him the invisible was so close! Had my revolt offended God so much that he had closed himself to me?

How old had I been—ten, twelve? A woman was dancing about the fire. A village festival. The drum fell silent. She was dancing on the embers. Light-footed, radiant, I shifted to see her better. I knew her well. She was not a sorceress. So? I began to tremble. Religious fear. The burden of the mystery. Around me all was meditative silence. She started to sing in an unknown tongue. My hands, my feet, my heart trembled. I was consumed by a desperate desire to resist that overwhelming magic. I made one sign of the cross after another. I was being taken by storm; my resistance wavered, my hesitations vanished. I found myself in the woman's embrace, shouting, shouting, dancing to unfamiliar music. "Last night you danced on the embers," she told me the next day. I had never believed it. The bad dream surged up again, insistent. If only God could overcome me so simply! Possess me!

"Fabrizio: do the truly possessed still exist?"

"I don't know, Pierre. It's not impossible. In his book on Satan's presence Monsignor Cristiani makes a good case for it."

"But the possessed are just sick."

"Of course, my dear fellow. But what is it in them that is sick?"

"I want to make my confession, Jacques."

Much relieved, he smiled. Yes, I thought, take me back. I'm delirious. I don't want to start all over again. I want to live as I used to, in outward calm and inner turmoil. Perhaps beyond language I can find the hope I seek, the sublime Reality. Sanguinetti appeared before me, regal: "He is the radiant and luminous Ocean, the Source of all Ideas, the Salvation and the Goal of the perceptible as of the imperceptible, the perfect Being constituted by his very Existence. The First, coextensive with the totality of Being, He is the Inexpressible, He is One, Holy, thrice Holy." The glory of God's peace drew me inexorably, in my weakness and misery. I trusted You, oh Lord, and You will not abandon me.

Jacques had shut his eyes. He is praying for me, I told myself, consoled, seeing myself received once again in the circle of Christly life. Yes: I will go in again to my father's house and live his life again in the Eucharist.

"Pierre, I should very much like to receive your confession. . . ." He was uneasy, obviously groping for the right words. "Pierre," he began again with a gentle glance, "you understand that . . . Do you regret what you have done?"

"No, Jacques. No regrets. On the contrary."

He seemed quite unhappy. "In that case I cannot give you absolution."

A wave of anger filled me; it ebbed as suddenly. Wild laughter shook me. "No, no, old friend, just leave me alone; alone, yes, alone."

I was laughing. Joy! He thinks, I said to myself, that I've gone crazy. So much the better.

15

I LEFT.

A deliberate indifference overrode my anguish. When I was quite small my grandmother told me again and again, *"Kajadikila beena bilowa, byenda bishala bisendama* (He is eager to rearrange others' calabashes, while his own lie any which way)." The proverb, surging up out of my childhood, had forced me to see myself as I was. Hadn't I been too sensitive to others' servility to understand the sharp detour on my own path?

Why go on seeking? I had been too much in love with poetry. That was what Jacques offered me in the hospital: the laws of love and hope, the coherence of an apostolate, and the ephemeral consolation of silent transsubstantiations. To accomplish these miracles all one had to do was believe, even reluctantly—but only after annihilating other faiths. So the stark moral purity I had aspired to was denied me. Jacques was offering me the fragility of phrases as celebration and portent of a dazzling eternity.

I was too tired. Theology, too simple in its symbolism;

prayer, too exhausting in my weakness. And I believed they'd destroyed my initiative forever. The language of a universe exceeded the reality of that same universe too ambitiously, too deceptively, too much to the benefit of the supernatural; my emotions would never be stirred again. I knew a bit about these ups and downs of the spirit. So the complexities of moral and intellectual duty no longer fazed me. Definitions like principles, postulates, deductions, inductions, and corollaries only frustrated my heart like disappointing legacies: unfortunate and worn out by the long pursuit.

To stay in hospital was, I thought, a hibernation. How could I extend it into the life to come?

Life is a strong force; true. And poetry too beautiful, despite the binding strength of time. I loved it in spite of everything. Perhaps that was why Eluard's durability inspired me. *Le dur désir de durer.* And I said to myself, "A woman is more beautiful than the world I live in."

Would my ancestors and my people finally approve of me? Ah, if I could only live without missing them so! That too is a fruitful path. I should have to be reborn. I am still young. In European terms—but so what? I am not even forty years old. "A bachelor can only be a man deprived by nature or by luck. A celibate is one of the damned." My evasions came to a natural end, and I found the ritual formula: "Tell this young woman that I desire her greatly."

Kaayowa. She came with her parents and her uncles. She lived with them. As a little girl, Kaayowa was a sorceress. So we had something in common. When she grew up, a Cimungu of Kadima's line came to marry her. That was Kadima called Mwamba. When Kongolo, chief of the Bena Cimungu, decided to open hostilities against the men of Cimuna, Mwamba wa Kadima died mysteriously. So Kaayowa was a sorceress. Drums conversed all night. Kaayowa became pregnant. The mystery deepened.

"She must die," said Kongolo, chief of the Cimungu. "She

must die, in full view of women like herself and of the children. The goats must watch her die; the dogs and chickens, the toads and all the insects must open their eyes to see how Kaayowa the sorceress dies." She did not die. The ancestors were afraid of her. They killed her child: Kaayowa gave birth to a stillborn son. Accursed, she fled the region. Kongolo, chief of the Bena Cimungu, said, "You were married; your uncles accepted the marriage portion, your parents the goats and chickens, and you yourself a hearth. Despite that, you killed your husband and child. You are a criminal. Your crimes upon you, go and die elsewhere. Like your ancestors, we cast you out. Go and die elsewhere, I said."

"Kaayowa, my sister, I shall love you. My friends, go and tell Kaayowa that I desire her." In saving her from the malediction, I would save my own soul. But it was Antoinette and Garbage Girl that I dreamed of. An ordinary life, just like the lives of other men of my race, would end the Satanic resonances of my soul. I would therefore create such a life.

With the tensions of celibacy eased, I was unhappy. I bore the weight of a world. My love was not even characteristic of my race. My intent still less so. The equality of the sexes. Shared love. Mutual sacrifices. The whole litany of sexual lyricism. I wondered in vain whether love among us was a communion or only the cause or effect of a communion. I held forth on the two hearts that beat as one—but I distanced myself fatally from real life. Kaayowa only existed. She was a silent receptacle. My hackneyed phrases meant nothing to her. I tempted her, luring her dangerously toward treacherous concepts.

"What does my master wish?"

"I am not your master, Kaayowa. I am your husband."

She stood mute. Then she left me, head bowed.

"Kaayowa, why do you eat by the fire? We should eat side by side."

"That is how I was taught, my lord. My place is not at the table."

"I am not your lord but your husband."

So our lives never intersected. The tradition of my own people deprived me of my last chance.

"Kaayowa, let us take a walk."

"But, Father, I cannot. My place is here by the hearth."

"Yes, you can. Furthermore, I am not your father."

"As you wish, lord."

She came along. It was painful. She walked five paces behind me. Tradition demanded it.

"Kaayowa, why do you never speak to me?"

"What could I say to you, my lord? You know that I must hear and obey."

Even the temptations of female companionship were never satisfactory. There was no real convergence. I had a slave. Her role was to exist, passive, in the service of a society which expected of her obedience, absolute discretion, and children. Our dull intimacy killed my dream. I thought of Eluard's wonderful line and understood too late. My celibacy in the service of a European priesthood had brewed the sickly languor of the allegory Botticelli painted for the Vespucci: Mars and Venus. It was another universe.

A tedious game. How long could it last? A few cries followed the brief amusement. Even eroticism was a dead end. Like the perversions I had learned in the confessional, my vices could not be shared. Indifferent, Kaayowa awaited the onset of my ecstasies, an object offered up in self-denial. Tradition forbade her to share them. That was a good wife. So the flesh lost its drunken urge rather quickly. Disgust replaced it and grew. From one day to the next . . . I dreamed of a college girl. She would have been more like me.

I had told the auxiliary bishop, "Jacques, after my time with the rebels I can't come back to you honestly."

"And why not?"

"Do you know any poor people?"

"I do indeed. We're surrounded by them."

"That's my race, Jacques. My new race. I want to go back
to my roots. I cannot live so far from them. The very odor of
poverty hangs about me."

"But my poor friend—"

"No, Jacques. That's the way it is. I'll live as they live."

"Rest now, my friend. You're exhausted, you know. Later,
we'll see."

The odor of poverty. Truth is, it disgusted me. I had no real wish
to go back to yams and beans. But I had to lie to Jacques, to
maintain the logic of my excursion among the guerrillas. All I
could allow myself from now on was to shake up the complacent.
So I needed a vocabulary to cloak my acts and desires. I loved
and understood the poor only in stylish revolutionary writings.
That was at least something. I needed at least that logical support to live without shame. But in fact, my flesh tormented me.
Conjugal life was irresistibly attractive. A real communion, lived
in daily observances of the flesh. The physical life. No, it was not
quite that. It was rather that the gap between normal daily life
and Thomist strictures seemed more than ever inconsequential.
And the sun was warming me again. That was the tropics: sunshine. I no longer really cared about the poor and the guerrillas.
If I'd still loved them I'd have turned mason or carpenter. Or
even road mender. I'd considered it for a time, to prick the
conscience of my bourgeois brother priests. Like a coward I told
myself I'd be more useful to the poor if I accepted a position of
responsibility. I was lying to myself. Did I fool my brother? He
helped me. I became principal private secretary in the Ministry
of Mining and Energy. My brother worried about me. "Pierre,
you're unreasonable."

"How?"

"About women. You can carry independence too far, you
know."

"No sir. If you knew what it was like to be the slave of
slogans, to spend years trying to love the Word . . ."

A silly game. Blasphemous. It seemed to vindicate me, and I was happy to cling to it as a refuge. Kaayowa disgusted me. When I saw that she was pregnant, fears assailed me again. And as joy rose among my people, panic rose within me.

"Finally living a real life! A child is important, Pierre."

A man without a child is a dead man.

Ancestral tradition sprang forth triumphant. I wanted to understand, but never worked through my own contradictions and discords. Their joy condemned me; it was the measure of my soul's treason.

That is why I hesitated. Did I understand any of this at all? And now I am struggling to suppress all hope of inner peace.

"I'm leaving."

My brother thought I meant a trip somewhere.

"No, I'm leaving for good."

"Where to, if you don't mind?"

"I don't know. But I'm leaving."

He blew up. Called me a failure, an idiot. He was right. I only wish his comprehensive insults had helped to define me.

"You're going back to the Church, aren't you?"

"But I never left it." After that confession of my own confusions, I begged him, "Try to understand me."

"You're crazy! With your wife pregnant? A fine time to leave!"

"But—"

"And you call yourself a priest!"

Yes, I called myself a priest. I had no conscience whatever. I knew that my wife would be cared for. My family would take her in. I wanted to be taken in as well, by my own family.

I had to save my soul: to preserve, at least and at any price, the despair of my meditations. So I left. This small Cistercian monastery, where I am relearning the rites, is not even a way station.

I have become a novice. Literally and figuratively. Have I found the right path? The fear of madness still haunts me. And

I have waited in vain for a judgment. Weary, I choose the lulling fluency of official institutions, the falsehood of catchwords. Shall I reach the truth by dint of lies?

The prior asked me, "Pierre Landu: what do you seek in this monastery?"

"Christ."

"Are you prepared to follow him according to our holy rule?"

"Yes, I am prepared."

I can't even be sure I was sincere during the ceremony of vestment. A Cistercian . . . in principle that was a new start toward Christ. But what does Christ still mean to me?

I recalled Venice. The gentle turbulence of early autumn had driven us toward the Bridge of Sighs. A ridiculous promenade among the flood of tourists. "Pietro, do you *find* Christ?"

"I don't know, Fabrizio."

"I suffer. He's a person to me. But only historic. I'd like to *live* Christ in adoration."

"I would too. But I try to find him in people. That's probably an easy way out."

Had that answer helped me? How would I do here? The lie, once agreed to, holds me in eternal expectation. Awaiting His return. But can I wait if I no longer hope? I go on reeling off words—not arguments or exercises, only words. Job: Man that is born of woman is of few days, and full of trouble.

The novitiate. Of course I'll complete it. And become a good Cistercian. One can accomplish anything. All one has to do is be logical about words and their meanings. I leaf through the works of our Father, Saint Bernard, supremely bored. More precisely, I scan them. Am astonished that there existed in this world a man who tolerated God's empty phrases because he encompassed Him so perfectly. . . . Three weeks ago the Stelae of Segalen, luminous religion, might have spelled the defeat of spirituality. I read through them and admire them as if they were a strikingly beautiful weapon suddenly become obsolete:

The Emperor—father of all beliefs, and honoring in each
of them the Reason which is One—wills that this, almost ef-
faced by neglect, be transcribed to a new tablet and marked
by the seal of his reign.

Is not the Admirable Being the Unity-Trinity, the Lord
without Origin, Oloho? He divided the world in the form of a
cross; released the primordial air; raised the heavens and the
earth; launched the sun and the moon; created the first man
in perfect harmony.

But Sa-Than gave out lies, proclaimed the equality of
the Powers and set the creature in place of the Eternal. Man
lost his way and could not find it again. Then came promises;
an incarnation; an agony; a death; a resurrection. Now it is
not good to reveal that to men.

Let no one therefore dare to add commentaries here. Let
no one seek instruction here. So that Luminous Belief may die
in peace and obscurity, with neither fruits nor disciples.

Saint Bernard's commentaries depress me more every day.
My break is clearly confirmed. And yet I am plunging deeper
than ever into the statelessness of divine glory. Distortions and
deformations: I am sacrificing the man to violent words because
people read them symbolically. Taking the cloth: the dreadful
degeneration of a philosophy, of a theology. During the whole
ceremony I was thinking about dishwater. An abstract art.

There it is: I am living this quite concrete art which, because it is made vivid by accelerating certain rhythms of life, is
improperly called abstract. Malevich's lectures: my way of taking
the cloth.

Aside from the monks here in the monastery, only Monsignor Jacques Matani linked me to ecclesiastical academe, and to
my race.

"My dear Brother Matthew: I owed you that."

I admired his powers of adaptation. With startling speed he
had acquired, from the bishop, the plumpness proper to the too
well fed, the automatic motion of a hand casually extended for a

kiss. We blacks, I decided, have the agility of monkeys. It is a great resource. The light betrayed me. Stravinsky's *Sacre du Printemps* was danced, for me alone, by black imps. Senseless perfection. I smiled bitterly.

"I am happy for you, Brother Matthew," he repeated.

The sun rode the skies, and with scandalous nonchalance I was committing myself to the European Middle Ages. He called me Brother Matthew. He had adapted, he who had always called me Pierre.

"Matthew-Mary of the Incarnation. That is henceforth your name. Pierre Landu in the secular world. You have died; learn now to live by the Gospels and the rule of our Father Saint Bernard. . . ."

I am like a pregnant woman. A new catchphrase redefined me. I agreed. I reel off the stupidly boring canonical hours knowing that for me they are only words. And the journey doesn't even tire me. Matthew-Mary of the Incarnation intones a hymn of joy. And breaks into a heavy sweat. . . .

"Brother Matthew, will you take my confession?"

"Yes, Monsignor, I'm listening."

The gestures came back to me, and the words. I listened to my own voice. Distancing myself from my conscience is the only pleasure I can still enjoy. My words worked a miracle. "Trust in Christ. With his guidance, I cannot doubt that you will arrive in his presence. God is your father: let that belief pervade. It is an extraordinary thing. God is your father. Never again fear anything." The words emerged mechanically. I heard myself conclude: *May Almighty God have pity on you, and after forgiving your sins may He lead you to eternal life.* . . . These magic formulas were a farewell to life. So then, my precious phrases, you have become my lackeys, Thanks to you, I live without surprises and without fuss. All vexation vanishes, sucked away by the silence of this place.

Reveal the true me? It isn't even a question of finding the right moment for it. Which moment? I am living in Christ. That is what matters. During meditation after lauds this morning, before the Solemn High Mass, I read a few passages of Simonov: *Days and Nights in Stalingrad.* They trimmed my fall and my serenity with happiness. A gripping moment. Was it really unforeseen? I'd believed that no love could ever again justify a death. Was that true? The men must stand fast. Not retreat one step. An order from the Führer. An order from the Marshal. Vilshofen, in command of the armor, has his general on the phone: "I believe you still have ammunition?" "Yes, General. A few rounds left for the rifles and mortars." "And you still have rations?" "Yes, sir. Today we have horsemeat soup and tomorrow we shall have more horsemeat soup." "Then go on defending your positions! I want your word as an officer!" "Yes, General. I give you my word as an officer." Until the horsemeat soup runs out, Vilshofen thought. Simonov, why is that hero's oath so depressing, that epic oath backed by a hero's psaltery? Horsemeat soup isn't bad. If horsemeat soup were the most you could be, you wouldn't be doing too badly.

"How do you feel now, Brother Matthew-Mary of the Incarnation?"

"Very well, thank you, Prior."

"And your prayers?"

"Cold and curt. I am the subject and the object of my own prayers. I find my nourishment in the profane."

"It is a gift of God, my son. Accept the emptiness."

"God is never within me."

"Are you sure of that, Brother? Apropos of the Word, our Father Saint Bernard wrote some marvelous pages about its presence in absence. Perhaps you know them already? For example:

Saint Bernard says:

When it enters in unto me the Word never betrays its presence by the slightest stirring, by the least sensation; only the secret trembling of my heart detects it. The inner man is re-

newed, and the Word is within me like the shadow of its splendor.

A sumptuous fatigue answers the prior's questing glance; in it he reads the mark of Providence. A fatigue impermeable to remorse as to resolve. I choose to remain a desert place, only a nothing comfortably ensconced in this setting so exotic to inhabitants of the real world. And what am I proving? I read a little Saint Bernard. His explosions of love, his furies, evoke not the least echo. They simply carry me back to the Middle Ages, attractive because so profoundly atheistic.

I must learn again to walk, head bowed, hands beneath the scapular. Bank any fire in my expression so that all may read in it the peace of Christ contemplated. Never run; never take the stairs two at a time. Become the image of patience. . . .

"Pierre Landu, our Father said one day, 'Nothing that touches God is alien to me.' Commit yourself to follow him in that. Your name is Matthew. That was the name of our Abbott: we have bestowed it upon you. Follow in the footsteps of that holy man, who had just left us for our Father's house. . . . Mary of the Incarnation, so that in our Order's spirit of spirituality you may endeavor your whole life long to be simply an imitation of the Virgin offered to the Divine Will."

Why should I shirk that? My choice is made. Why yield to recrimination? It would be awkward to denounce the obsessions of my heart. The tomb suits me perfectly. The gift of words . . . The canonical hours, strung out along the day, are a cycle of words of life. They come at stated times and I give my responses in chorus.

. . . Pierre Landu . . . No, I am Matthew-Mary of the Incarnation— What a falling-off is there! No, rather what glory! A place for everyone and everyone in his place. I am steeping myself in the Church's past to become a prayer offered up to the present. . . . The Church's past, or Europe's? It's the same thing. I accept. Faith is precisely that absurdity— Not the innocence of the slave? No; primitive impulses— You are the incarnation of sacrilege and blasphemy— No doubt. But by imitating prayer I shall one day become prayer— Offered up to God; and if my God is myself, my anguish will bring me closer to my own center— It's cowardly— God is merciful— Who is He? He is mercy— Those are only words— Isn't everything only words? You've chosen fluency— Yes, in nonsense. That's the gift of beginnings.

My dialogues have become self-defense. I refuse absolutely to violate the strict certainty that I consist wholly of an appalling hatred. To abandon that certainty would be to kill the man. For whose benefit? The black in me will die his sweet death. The pro-Marxist student has diluted himself in temptations of the flesh. Only my hate survives, in and with the complicity of words.

A sad happiness, but at least sure. I see the hours approach like polite glances. I contemplate myself, judge myself, and condemn myself. To consummate this torture in utter self-abnegation, to offer that self to the remote and invisible God of my dreams as a poor child, such is the perversity of my faith. Can I be saved by the distance I must keep in order to recognize myself as a traitor?

It was a winter evening. Fabrizio was sick. I went to see him.

"I want to die, Pierre."

"Fabrizio! That's not a thing to wish for, is it? It's a lack of Faith."

"No, I have Faith; I believe I have. That's why I want to die."

"What does Faith mean to you?"

"It means, *Credo quia absurdum.*"

The sky was lowering. I think of Africa's blue sky. Can all the vast life inexpressible in words justify Faith? "But Teilhard de Chardin has shown us how to believe even if we base belief on a scientific vision of life."

"They talk about that a lot; far too much. It's a theodicy for

bank presidents. That kind of marriage of convenience to mod-
ernize the Church is no new thing. Fact is, their theories betray
the Faith; they're condemned in advance. No, Pietro, Teilhard
de Chardin does not have Faith. One must believe because it is
absurd! That is the only path to salvation. . . . Look at the
apostles. A stranger tells them that he is God. . . ."

The endless rolling swell of mountains, to the very horizon . . . The sun is still shining. Almost four o'clock. I go to
make my preparations, to wash my face, to don my scapular. The
clock will strike for vespers.

I drift among currents. Is it fresh water? The throb of drums
scarcely ripples its surface. The mud and mire are far away. The
Gregorian chant will soar, a river of virtue sustained by the
human voice. The voice.

"I was at matins this morning," Monsignor Matani told me.
"What an act of faith! To see you there stretching toward
heaven, rising, kneeling, bowing all together, I feel so close to
God, so close. . . ."

Is he guilty? I don't even envy him. Which is why I dared
not shock him by telling him that throughout the service I was
humiliated. As, by the way, I am always. I always think of my
closest colleagues—haunted as I am by the horror of their sweat-
ing bodies. I answered courteously, playing by the rules: "Yes,
Monsignor, if only we could become living prayers, our happiness would be complete."

Two minutes to four. I must hurry. I shall be late. My poor
self-deceptions go on. Exalting in the expectation of a Messiah
who may never come again. My only grace is that duplicity, that
imitation of love, still embedded in my heart, inviting me to
melt altogether into the glory and debauchery of empty symbols.
What a tapestry! But on the other hand, what a glory for man
that he can be so humble in his very baseness!